On Zeb

"I sailed with Zeb quite a few times and it was always a memorable experience."

—James Cagney, one of the great actors of the twentieth century and frequent summer visitor on Martha's Vineyard

"He was one of the finest seamen navigating the waters from Nova Scotia to New Jersey. . . . He could forecast a blow hours in advance and could tell the speed of the schooner by merely looking over the side. He knew Long Island Sound so well, all you had to do was give him a few soundings and he could tell you where you were in a dense fog and how long it would be before the next mark could be picked up."

—Charlie Marthinusen, a native of Norway who spent his life at sea and was Zeb's mate for fifteen years

"Among schooner men, Zeb was a classic. Among schooners, Zeb's *Alice S. Wentworth* was a classic. Among the books on schooners, and schoonermen, Polly Burroughs's *Zeb* remains a classic. In telling the story of Zeb and his world, she vividly captures life on the New England coast in a time past."

—J. Revell Carr, Director Emeritus, Mystic Seaport

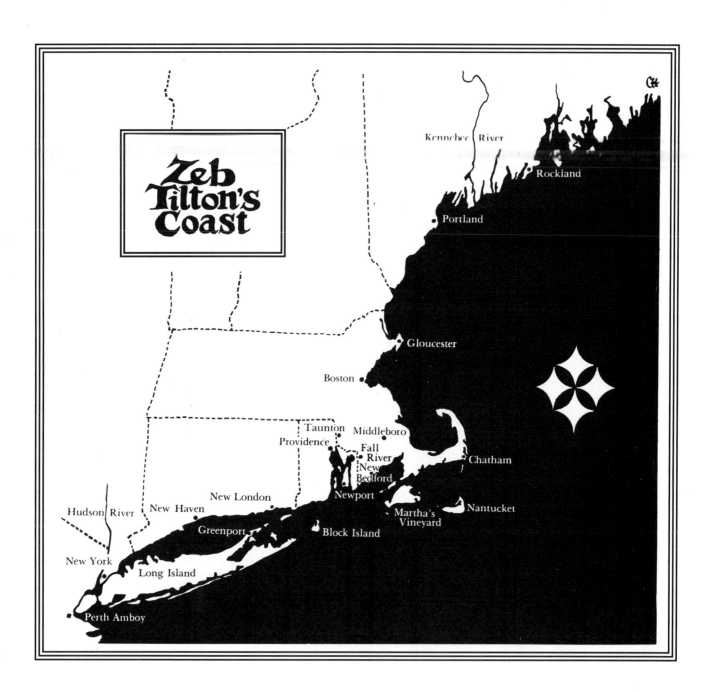

Zeb Tilton's Coast

Kennebec River

Rockland

Portland

Gloucester

Boston

Taunton · Middleboro
Providence · Fall River
New Bedford · Chatham
Newport
Martha's Vineyard · Nantucket
New London
New Haven
Hudson River
Greenport · Block Island
New York
Long Island
Perth Amboy

ZEB

CELEBRATED SCHOONER CAPTAIN
OF MARTHA'S VINEYARD

Polly Burroughs

INSIDERS' GUIDE®

GUILFORD, CONNECTICUT
AN IMPRINT OF THE GLOBE PEQUOT PRESS

A · **TWODOT**® · **BOOK**

INSIDERS' GUIDE ®

Copyright © 2005 by Polly Burroughs

Cover design: Bill Brown

Front cover photo: Zebulon Tilton at the wheel of the *Alice S. Wentworth*, *The Standard-Times*, New Bedford, collection of the author. Back cover images, clockwise from left: Captain Zebulon Northrop Tilton, photo by Louis Davidson, courtesy of Charles F. Sayle; Edgartown Harbor at the end of the nineteenth century, Martha's Vineyard Historical Society; the *Alice S. Wentworth* under way, Charles F. Sayle.

Text design: Christopher Harris
Library of Congress Cataloging-in-Publication Data is available.

ISBN 0-7627-3842-1

Manufactured in the United States of America
First Edition/First Printing

ACKNOWLEDGMENTS

It would have been impossible to tell the story of Zeb Tilton without the cooperation of those who worked, laughed, and lived with him—a man who was one of the most unforgettable characters on Martha's Vineyard. Since the book was originally published in 1972, almost everyone who contributed so much to Zeb's story has died. Their invaluable contributions live on, however, as does the old skipper's place in American maritime history.

I am particularly grateful to Henry Hough, who first suggested Zeb's story to me, and to Gale Huntington, without whom the book could not have been written.

While the historical details of Zeb's life are certainly true, no one can be entirely sure exactly when and where he made his salty, hilarious remarks. In each case, Zeb's wording has been supplied by a direct witness or the person to whom the remark was made, such as his mates, family, or friends.

I am deeply indebted to the following persons for having been so patient when I was writing the book, and who submitted to having their memories jogged again and again: Charles Sayle; John Leavitt; James Cagney; Katherine Cornell; Joseph Case Allen; Cyril Norton; Sydney Harris; Roy Campbell; and Zeb's mates Walter Jenkinson, Manuel Sylvia, and Charlie Marthinusen.

I also wish to thank those who generously searched for their old photographs, without which the book would have been incomplete: Charles Sayle for his superb collection; Murray and Roger Peterson of Maine; Bill Merry for his father's excellent collection; Mrs. Ralph Packer for her scrapbook; Clara Dinsmore; Mrs. Denys Wortman; Mrs. Gould; and Alfred Eisenstaedt, whose superb photos speak for themselves.

The following newspapers and organizations also played an important part in putting Zeb's story together: the *Vineyard Gazette;* the Martha's Vineyard Historical Society; *The Standard-Times,* New Bedford; the Old Dartmouth Historical Society; the Peabody Museum; the Newport Historical Society; the *Providence Journal;* the Staten Island Historical Society; the Brooklyn Public Library; South Street Seaport Maritime Museum; the Museum of the City of New York; the Rhode Island Historical Society; and the United States Coast Guard Academy.

Members of Zeb's family were extremely helpful: Zeb's nephews Tom and Alton Tilton, both of whom spent some time on the *Wentworth;* Zeb's daughter Rosalie Spence, who shared her memories and invaluable family photographs; Zeb's granddaughter Rosalie Spence Bernard, who sailed with Zeb as a child; and Mildred Huntington, Zeb's niece, who also sailed with her uncle.

I would also like to thank the book's original editor, Chris Harris, and Danquole Budris and Connie Scott; thanks as well to editors Laura Strom and Mimi Egan of The Globe Pequot Press for their invaluable help with this edition.

FOR NICHOLAS AND HANNAH

CONTENTS

LEFT: Captain Zebulon Northrop Tilton. *Photo: Louis Davidson, courtesy of Charles F. Sayle.* BELOW: The *Alice S. Wentworth* under way in 1938. *Photo: Charles F. Sayle.*

ZEB AND THE *ALICE*

On a brisk August afternoon in the 1930's, the *Alice S. Wentworth* came shouldering into Vineyard Haven Harbor in a good working breeze. The old schooner's topmast was bent like a coachwhip, straining to the pull of her grey, patched canvas. Her lee scuppers were smothered in a flurry of foam.

As she rounded the outer mark and headed up-harbor, the mate took in the topsail and dropped the flying jib. Several hundred yards off the pier he doused the jib, then the foresail. The captain timed the power of wind and water, pacing his sea-room and drift to the second, as he swung the two-master around. She slipped up towards the steamboat wharf, her mainsail coming down on the run. The mate had the fast line ready and curled it over a spile, as the *Wentworth* eased alongside and gently nudged the wharf.

He then jumped ashore to put out dock lines and returned to furl the sails. The skipper, Captain Zebulon Tilton, a huge, cross-eyed man, lean and leathered from his years at sea, untied the lines holding his cargo of lumber athwartship. He grabbed a bundle of pine boards, which would ordinarily have taken two men to handle, and swung them onto the steamboat wharf. Swiftly the lumber came off the deck. The mate then removed the forward hatch and jumped below to pass up the kegs of nails in her hold.

Scarred and blistered from her years at sea, the *Alice S. Wentworth* smelled of tar, hemp and the smoke which curled out of her soot-stained stack from the iron cookstove below. She was nearly the same age as her skipper, at least as craggy in appearance and surely as seaworthy.

The last of the kegs were coming out of the hold when a youthful itinerant preacher, thin as a shotten herring, approached and hailed the schooner.

"What can I do for you?" Zeb asked, as he straightened out, leaned against the rigging and wrapped his left hand around his chin.

"I'm asking for only fifty cents," mumbled the preacher.

"And why should I give you fifty cents?" inquired Zeb. His crossed eyes centered a little more than usual, an indication he was "thinking deep."

"It's for the Lord," answered the preacher.

"Young feller, how old be you?"

"Thirty," was the solemn reply.

"Well, Mister, I'm over sixty, You better give me the fifty cents for the Lord. I'll see Him first." With a ghost of a smile, the skipper turned backed to unloading.

It's been many years since Zeb took his fifty cents to the Lord, and his *Alice* is no more. But in their day, Zeb and *Alice* were known in every port from Maine to New York. His strength was immense, his sensitivity to the weather and to the sea was uncanny, and his wry Yankee wit was widely renowned. As a sailor, he had no peer. The *Wentworth* was the smartest, slipperiest coaster afloat; no schooner of equal size ever outsailed her. And with Zeb at the helm, it was said she could make Chicago on a heavy dew.

It was a perfect marriage, and unlike his three mortal wives and the countless women who found his curious charms irresistible, the *Alice S. Wentworth* had a hold on Zeb that no woman could ever achieve. If it came to a choice, and he doubtless hoped it never would, the sound of her canvas bellying out to a fair breeze had more allure than the rustle of any taffeta petticoat.

Still, Zeb was all of fifty-four before she became his alone, though they had had a brief affair a few years earlier. The full story really begins well before the turn of the century when Zeb was growing up on Martha's Vineyard Island, off the coast of Massachusetts.

II

THE SINGING TILTONS

It was the best of times on Martha's Vineyard Island when Zeb was growing up. The island's five ports and two inland villages were self-sufficient fishing, farming and whaling communities, intimately linked to the encircling, restless sea which had not only shaped the island's triangular contours but molded her history as well. With protected harbors, abundant fish and shellfish alongshore, and plenty of open space inland for agriculture, sheep and cattle grazing, a snug, uncomplicated way of life prevailed for the singularly hardy and independent Vineyard population.

Edgartown, the oldest village on the island, was a busy port engaged in shipping and whaling; it had become clear a century after the island's founding in 1641 that its wealth would come from the sea. Although whaling in general had begun to decline after the Civil War, Edgartown was still an active fitting-out port for the small local fleet as well as for the remaining Nantucket whaleships. The harbor at Nantucket, unlike Edgartown, was no longer deep enough to accommodate the vessels of progressively larger and larger dimensions required for the worldwide pursuit of the whale. Vineyard men, too, were in demand to serve as officers and crew. The success of their voyages was clearly evident from the numbers of ship chandlers, coopers, blacksmiths, shipwrights and bakers who operated around the waterfront. Large, stately captains' houses lined the streets up from the harbor. The handsome structures with gracious doorways, often crowned by fan-shaped windows, reflected the elegance which the profits from whaling afforded.

In the 1870's a railroad ran from Edgartown along the shore northerly to Cottage City (now called Oak Bluffs) which had a personality distinctly its own. Originally a campground for revival meetings, it had also become a summer resort with cottages, hotels and boarding houses trimmed in Victorian fretwork.

The principal port of Vineyard Haven, on the island's northwest corner was only five miles from the mainland across Vineyard Sound, a major crossroads of north-south shipping in the 1870's. Daniel Webster, one of the island's first renowned tourists, called it "the greatest and busiest sea lane in the world with the possible exception of the English Channel." Brigs, barks, schooners and sloops moving up and down the coast stood in on the sound for a landfall, or put in to the harbor to wait out a storm, make repairs, replenish supplies or wait for the tide. Like outstretched arms, the twin headlands of the Vineyard's East and West Chop cradled the harbor and protected it

13

LEFT: A bathing beach at Cottage City in the 1880s. *Photo: Marshall R. Cook Studio.* OPPOSITE, ABOVE: Vineyard Haven Harbor. The Crocker harness factory is at the left and the Seamen's Bethel is at the far right. *Courtesy of the Vineyard Gazette.* BELOW, LEFT: A well-turned-out cattle farmer up-island. *Photo: Marshall R. Cook Studio.* BELOW, RIGHT: William Manter and his wife Rebecca, who operated Manter's Mill at Roaring Brook. *Courtesy of the Vineyard Gazette.*

from all but a northeaster. Along the waterfront below the church-crowned town of white clapboard houses, a harness shop, shipyard, sail lofts, general stores and ship chandlers served the incoming vessels.

Between the small port at Menemsha Creek and the towering Gay Head Cliffs at the western tip lay Lobsterville, the most important seasonal fishing village on the island in the age of oar and sail. During the summer months fishermen, occupying shacks clustered alongshore, sold their fish and lobsters at five cents apiece to the smacks arriving daily from New York.

The mid-island towns of Chilmark and West Tisbury were picturesquely endowed with windswept moors, great ponds held behind barrier beaches, and winding dirt lanes leading down to coves where salt hay stood ready to be cut. Grey, weathered houses dotted the high, rolling land where miles of undulating stone walls confined the sheep and cattle. Here on the uplands where the land narrows, a farmer could rest his plow and view Vineyard Sound on the north and the magnificent sweep of the blue Atlantic to the south where breakers fringed the beaches and offshore bursts of white marked the foaming shoals. The echo from the thundering waves carried far inland.

Islanders got their salt from the sea, their rum and molasses from the West Indies, and their imagination from the dying embers of those long, wild winter nights. They grew vegetables, wove cloth, salted fish, and shot wild turkey, heath hen and geese. They harvested and preserved the fruit, fashioned farm tools on the anvil, cut firewood and cleared the pastureland. Wary of mainlanders and contemptuous of the continent in general, they were the epitome of Yankee independence. The tales of their fierce individualism are legendary.

It is said that one of Zeb's ancestors slept on a bed under which he had stored his coffin and an appropriately engraved headstone. He trusted no one else's taste or literary judgment and apparently wished to settle the matter before it was beyond his control. The epitaph read: "Here lies the body of Jonathan Tilton/Whose friends reduced him to a skeleton/They wronged him out of all he had/And now rejoice that he is dead." To Jonathan, it all rhymed.

A story of another Vineyarder describes his introduction to a distant English relative who, he had heard, was fat, pompous and spoke with a strange accent. The fisherman stepped off his boat without raising his eyes. "Distant relatives are like distant

16

Four contemporary yet timeless Vineyard scenes: an up-island farmhouse; the sparkling surf at the Chilmark beach; sheep pastured on the south shore; and a silent lagoon. *Photos: Alfred Eisenstaedt.*

LEFT: The old Manter's Mill in North Tisbury. *Courtesy of the Vineyard Gazette.* BELOW: The unveiling of the Civil War Monument at Cottage City. OPPOSITE: Typical Vineyard trotting races. *Both, Martha's Vineyard Historical Society.*

thunder—the farther off the better," he muttered stomping by the visitor with his head lowered.

Inconsistency was accepted and even welcomed, often with enthusiasm. No one seems to have been startled by the Civil War Monument in Cottage City. After a large crowd had turned out for its dedication the American flag was snatched off with rich rhetorical flourish, unveiling a statue of a Confederate soldier. It is undoubtedly the only such monument to be erected at that time north of the Mason-Dixon Line.

Families frequently moved up- or down-island in a relaxed and unperturbed manner. A man not only took his wife, children and possessions, but with the aid of oxen, his house went with him, too. Personal feuds were commonplace; there were some who refused to speak to each other for years. On Chappaquiddick, if a man quarreled with his neighbor, he started the family burial ground on the property line, knowing that no self-respecting person would dare to tread on a grave.

Inter-town rivalries sometimes cropped up over boundaries. Although Eastville was geographically a part of East Chop, politically it was part of Edgartown. When some Edgartownians came over to work on a new road, an East Chop resident groaned, "It's a caravan from Hell." But they seemed to bury their differences at the West Tisbury trotting races, or the Agricultural Fair, held after the crops were in and the root cellars and larders were filled for the winter. And on one subject there was always agreement: the mainland and the mainlanders were to be regarded with suspicion and disdain.

But the seafaring men of the Vineyard were not so independent that they didn't attempt to make the most of the increased maritime shipping brought about by the Industrial Revolution. Over fifty thousand sail a year, by daylight count, passed through Vineyard Haven Harbor. The fish, wool and other island products were exported; whaling continued to be profitable; piloting was keen and competitive in Vineyard Haven; and waterfront business was flourishing.

The *Vineyard Gazette* reflected these prospering times when it advertised the latest in silk hats, Edison's new talking machine, Nevis rum for a dollar a gallon and Dr. Pierce's Pleasant Purgative Pellets to cure all derangements of the stomach and bowels. (One irate woman called the paper a "filthy little sheet" for printing such vulgarity, but she was ignored.)

OPPOSITE: *A contemporary Chilmark vista. Photo: Samuel Chamberlain, courtesy of Peabody Essex Museum.* RIGHT: *An up-island farm before the turn of the 20th century. Collection of the author.*

A give-away scheme usually enjoyed immense popularity. Besides their pots, pans, trinkets and bonnets, pack peddlers sometimes offered one acre of land to anyone buying their patent medicine. The so-called shorefront property, which might come with a kidney cure, was actually in mid-island, but many happily fell for the "medicine lot" plan anyway.

It was here on this small, rugged island, on a farm off Old North Road, that Zebulon Northrop Tilton was born. The date was December 1, 1866. His ancestors had emigrated to the New World from England in the 1660's, and for six generations Tilton men had been farmers, whalers, fishermen and merchant sailors.

Zeb had three older brothers, William, Welcome and George Fred, and three younger, John R., Edward Van Buren and Willard, as well as a sister, Flora. All had red hair except Zeb, whose hair was brown, and all had high cheekbones, said to be inherited from an Indian ancestor.

A story about John Lawrence Tilton, one of Zeb's bachelor uncles, admirably illustrates another family trait. In his youth, whenever he came off a schooner in Boston Harbor, John Lawrence often visited a certain waterfront saloon also frequented by John Sullivan, the lightweight boxing champion of Massachusetts (not to be confused with John L. Sullivan, the heavyweight). Although not as large as most of the family, Tilton was made of the same steel and possessed the same rapid reflexes. He also dressed impeccably and cut quite a swath in his fawn-colored trousers and figured waistcoat. Sullivan, in turn, was noted for his belligerence which was said to increase in direct proportion to his alcoholic intake. On this occasion the boxer, who had an aversion to fancy clothes, sidled up to Tilton and mashed his fine hat down on his head.

"I wa'n't do that if I was you," the wiry Vineyarder quietly warned him. Again Sullivan slapped him on the head, bringing his hat down around his ears. "I said I wa'n't do that if I was you," Tilton warned him again in his most dignified manner. Silence fell in the barroom and all eyes riveted on the islander. Tilton turned to his companion and said, "If you see to fair play, I think I'll just take a round out of that feller." Before the words were out of his mouth he felt the boxer's hand come down again on his head. Instantly Tilton turned and swung—his reach was perfect—and the lightweight boxing champion of Massachusetts lay on the barroom floor.

The saloon regulars took up a collection to show their gratitude and the proprietor

OPPOSITE: A mid-island pine forest. *Photo: Alfred Eisenstaedt.* RIGHT: Wind-driven snow attacks a Vineyard barn. *Photo: Shirley Mayhew, courtesy of the Vineyard Gazette.*

offered to hire him as a bouncer. John Tilton graciously thanked the saloonkeeper, but declined, saying, "I like a taste of rum now and again, but I wa'n't want to swim in it."

The Tilton farm of several hundred acres was jointly owned by John Lawrence Tilton, another bachelor uncle Ainsworth, and Zeb's father, George Oliver Tilton. Ainsworth was noted for bathing naked in the brook by his house all year round, claiming the waters of the stream had therapeutic values never found in a well. His constant diet of thinly sliced raw pork and semi-boiled potatoes carried him to an old age. It is said that John and Ainsworth occasionally disagreed over housekeeping standards. One evening a section of the kitchen stovepipe broke and John complained bitterly to Ainsworth about the choking smoke. When Ainsworth paid no attention, John knocked the lid out of Ainsworth's silk top hat and substituted the crown for the broken pipe.

While Ainsworth could ignore a smoke-filled room, he was meticulous about the floors. Whenever enough wood ashes had accumulated in the stove, he would spread them over the whole first floor of the house and sprinkle it down with water. After letting the whole mess soak in for a time, he would sweep it up and shovel it out the window, thoroughly convinced that there was no finer wood preservative than lye from wood ashes.

While raising sheep up-island could provide a prosperous living, dirt farming was apt to be on a subsistence level. Nonetheless, Zeb's father, George Oliver, chose to support his family by growing potatoes and vegetables, while occasionally digging and selling the kaolin clay on the north shore. The clay was loaded aboard coastal schooners at the wharf near Paint Mill Brook for shipment to the New Bedford and Somerset potteries. Zeb's father also went cod fishing in spring and fall, mainly to supply his family, though in a particularly good season he would sell the surplus. George Oliver was a fine boatman; he made it a point to take his sons out for cod at an early age, teaching them the rudiments of fishing and handling a small craft in all weather. Their income was irregular; but to George Oliver, who was a casual, easygoing man, and to his wife Hannah, this was an acceptable way of life.

Their home was a loosely constructed, oak-framed, story-and-a-half, shingled house. In the attic a couple of rooms for the children were partitioned off from the rest of the unfinished space. On a winter's morning the Tilton youngsters were quite used to turning out barefoot on a floor covered with snow driven through the shingles.

Fishing boats off Gay Head. *Left photo: Samuel Chamberlain, courtesy of Peabody Essex Museum.*
Right photo: W.O. Richards, courtesy of the Vineyard Gazette.

Schooners clearing Vineyard Haven Harbor
near the turn of the 20th century. *Courtesy of*
the Vineyard Gazette.

A winter storm. *Courtesy of the Vineyard Gazette.*

THE SEA IN MANY MOODS FROM THE MARTHA'S VINEYARD COAST.

Schooner yachts, coasting schooners and sloops rounding Cottage City headed for Edgartown in the 1880s. *Photo: Marshall R. Cook Studio.*

The Chilmark Methodist Church and parsonage, which George Oliver Tilton's family attended. *Martha's Vineyard Historical Society.*

The schoolhouse in 1971. *Photo: Christopher Harris.* OPPOSITE. An aged Edgartown barn. *Photo: Samuel Chamberlain,* courtesy of Peabody Essex Museum.

The one-room school nearby had spring and fall terms only. Classes were usually taught by the oldest girl who had graduated the previous term. This kept the "town's money at home"—a trait beloved by Vineyarders. When not in school, the children picked ed blueberries and cranberries in the swamp or in George Oliver's bog near his house, receiving one and a half cents a quart. They also gathered oysters in the salt ponds and dug clams in the bays.

They were a high-spirited, undisciplined clan who thought little about the future, being in tune only with the turn of the seasons which supplied what little variety spiced their lives. The children ran wild over the fields and into neighbors' barns, playing with wooden swords in the hay, climbing, jumping, and creating noisy mischief all the while.

Their nearest neighbors, one Captain Hammet and his wife, were themselves childless and thus accustomed to a precise and orderly life which the eight carefree Tilton children could not help but regularly upset.

One day Flora found a perfectly round cowflop in the pasture, almost the exact size of a three-layer cake and dry enough for handling. She took the meadow-muffin home and carefully and secretly frosted it, adding a few precious store-bought gumdrops for decoration. At dusk, she and her brothers crept over to the Hammets, placed the cake on the step, banged on the door and fled.

The Hammets' fury, as usual, must have fallen on deaf ears, for George Oliver was a jovial man who lived one day at a time and didn't consider his children's pranks important. He was, however, deeply religious and a pillar of the Chilmark Methodist Church. The family regularly traveled, either on foot or by wagon, the two and a half miles to attend the Sunday morning services and the Wednesday night prayer meetings. In between, George Oliver took his evening Bible reading very seriously indeed, though he constantly complained about the lack of suitable spectacles. He tried several pairs from the general store and had even ordered others from an ad in the *New England Homestead*, all without success. One day Zeb brought home a beautiful pair from which he had carefully removed the lenses. George Oliver was sitting by the fire reading the Bible and complaining about his glasses as usual.

"Try these, Pa," Zeb suggested.

George Oliver put them on and looked up at his huge boy with a pleased smile. "Son, them there is perfect," he said.

Three of Zeb's brothers. LEFT to RIGHT: George Fred, as a boy, *courtesy of Rosalie Tilton Spence;* William, taken about 1930; and Welcome, aged 90, with his wife Hattie, *both couresty of Emily Huntington Rose.*

The Tiltons' life in the evenings, as elsewhere on the island, centered around the kitchen hearth most of the year. Often friends came around and the fishermen would sit by the fire repairing their nets while the women would knit. More often than not there'd be singing. For generations seafaring men had brought home songs from their long voyages at sea, and it was not uncommon to harmonize around the hearth where little encouragement was needed to start a musical time.

George Oliver's boys were known as the "Singing Tiltons" or the "North Road Tiltons," to distinguish them from the "South Road," "Middle Road" and "Down-Island" Tiltons. In spite of their isolation they were celebrated the length and breadth of the Vineyard for their voices.

If any one of them woke in the night and felt like vocalizing, he'd go downstairs, stoke up the fire and sing. One by one, others attracted to the sounds of "Rollin' Home," "Tarpaulin Jacket," "The Parlor," or Zeb's favorite, "Granny's Old Arm Chair," would appear until the whole family had gathered round. In laughter and song, they would carry on until sunrise, completely oblivious to any sense of time.

Some said they were the laziest family on the island because they never got up and never went to bed. Still, the boys had to leave home at an early age to go to work. There would be fewer mouths to feed, jobs were plentiful, and the money they made was always needed at home.

28

An ageless Vineyard still-life. *Photo: W.O. Richards, courtesy of the Vineyard Gazette.*

Zeb's brother, George Fred, went whaling and lived up to the family's extraordinary reputation for strength and courage. When the whaling fleet was trapped in the ice at Point Barrow, Alaska, in 1898, George Fred volunteered to walk the two thousand miles down the coast to seek help. He later wrote a book, *George Fred Himself*, describing this adventure.

William, following his innate talents, took to ditty singing and became a chantey-man on square-rigged ships.

In the years when the children were still young—if the crops and demand for clay were good—the family lived high for a while. Other times they had barely enough to eat, the basic diet being salt cod and turnip, or one of the precious chickens. The children either wore hand-me-down shoes or went without. During the lean winters, when the boys were out in the barn milking, they'd step in fresh cow manure to warm their feet.

The third oldest boy was born during a particularly bad time. The potato crop had failed the summer before, demand for clay had vanished and the barn had blown down during a severe winter gale. Because of this, the one cow that was fresh was stabled in the front parlor. When George Oliver first saw his new son, who had just been patted into life athwart the stern, the proud father explained to his hefty-lunged baby, "It's hard times here son, but you're welcome." The name stuck. Welcome shipped out on a

whaler when he was thirteen, though he quickly turned to coasting and fishing, explaining to Zeb, "The cabin boy (on a whaler) got paid off in silver. They tossed it through the rounds of a ladder and all what stuck to the rounds belonged to me. It wa'n't much. And they only served pie twice—once't when we cleared New Bedford and again when we was nearly home. The pie was thick as a piece of paper and I was never able to figure out what 'twas. Had one of those flavors you can't taste. You had to listen for it, but I couldn't hear nothin'."

Zeb's younger brother, John R., sang and did a little fishing, but never attended school. Flora, the only girl, distinguished herself by never singing a note. Edward Van Buren was one of the "strange Tiltons" (another family trait, though fortunately not a common one), and never went to sea or to school either. In fact, he never did anything but sing Gospel if he could help it. He was known as the "Chilmark Singer" at every isolated farm on Martha's Vineyard, Cape Cod and Nantucket. He could often be seen walking from Gay Head, where he might have visited some Indian friends, to Vineyard Haven some twenty miles distant, singing all the way. If it was a still day he could be heard a half a mile off. He was always polite and well received, exchanging local news and a few chores for a free meal and a haystack or barn in which to sleep.

Of the seven boys, Zeb was the strongest and the wittiest—he'd inherited his father's sense of humor and then some. His quiet chuckle was unlike the hearty laughter of his brothers, but his humor was sharp and never cruel. Zeb was also the homeliest son, burdened with the handicap of crossed eyes which he often joked about, claiming, "I got the advantage; I can see both ways at once." All the Tiltons were huge, but Zeb was enormous. He blamed his size on his father who, he claimed, sent him over the hill when he was a boy and told him not to return until he could see back over the top!

Zeb was just fifteen when he walked the ten miles to Vineyard Haven to sign aboard the two-masted coasting schooner *Eliza Jane*, of which Captain Josiah Cleveland was the master. The year was 1882.

The Vineyard Haven waterfront. LEFT: A variety of coastal schooners. *Courtesy of the Vineyard Gazette.* BELOW, LEFT: The Bethel boat *Helen Mary,* which brought seamen ashore from the fleet. *Courtesy of Thomas Hale.* BELOW, RIGHT: The steamer *Island Home.* BOTTOM: Heavy traffic under sail. *Both, Martha's Vineyard Historical Society.*

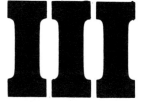

ZEB AND THE *ELIZA JANE*

The smaller schooners which linked all the northeastern coastal ports and off-shore islands didn't have the glamour of the deepwater ships which voyaged around Cape Horn to Australia and the Orient. Nonetheless, these fore-and-afters often took greater risks in contending with New England's shoals and erratic weather. Beamy, but fast and weatherly, the schooners could sail in shallow bays, choppy sounds, and up winding rivers so narrow there was barely space to turn around. Deepwater men often accused coastwise sailors of setting their course by the bark of a dog. The small vessels did have an obviously closer identity with the land than the packets or whalers which were at sea for years at a time. Still, their skippers took at least an equal amount of pride in a good passage and in the quality of their craft. Schooner captains had to be alert to every advantage of wind and tide in the fierce competition for cargoes. The off-shore islanders were completely dependent on the coasters to supply them with all the items they didn't make or grow themselves, such as nails, spices, molasses and tea. The islanders also needed to export their salt fish, wool, quahaugs, and cranberries.

When Zeb arrived at the waterfront, Vineyard Haven must have seemed the whole universe. Paddlewheelers were taking on passengers at the steamboat wharf. Bum-boats sailed in and out to meet incoming vessels selling everything from potatoes to socks. Dories moved back and forth; slatting canvas thundered impatiently to be furled; kegs clattered along the wharves; and the shouts of sailors aloft and ashore were carried about by salty breezes tinged with the smell of tar, oakum, fish and cordage.

Up on the West Chop shore was a Seamen's Bethel which catered to the sailor-man's soul, but it was scarcely a match for the streetwalkers who appeared the minute the fleet was in. Though there were no brothels as such in these smaller ports, the sail-ors coming ashore could find the girls quicker than they could scramble up the ratlines. Likewise, on the East Chop shore, known locally as the "Barbary Coast," a sailor had no trouble finding an evening's entertainment.

Zeb, for the first time in his life, could closely examine the huge three- and four-masters and watch the crews at work, two men to a mast. These great cargo carriers were the last word in economical, efficient transportation. They had evolved when the two-masted schooner grew so large in both sail and cargo capacity that to reef down its enormous canvas was a superhuman task. Many times these monstrous vessels had been blown far off the coast because their exhausted crews were unable to handle the

OPPOSITE: The four-masted Nova Scotia lumber schooner *Cutty Sark. Photo: © Mystic Seaport, Rosenfeld Collection, Mystic, CT.* ABOVE, LEFT: Perhaps the only photo of the *Eliza Jane,* seen at the far left, at anchor in Vineyard Haven Harbor. ABOVE, RIGHT: Captain Josiah Cleveland in his workshop about 1890. *Both courtesy of Charles F. Sayle.*

sails before a hard gale. As a result, shipwrights began building schooners with one or two additional masts so that the sail area could be divided into more manageable proportions. With the addition of donkey engines to raise and lower sail, four-masters were constructed to accommodate even larger cargoes. It was said they were "built by the mile and sawed off to suit the owner's pleasure." Such ships were often the property of a syndicate, or corporation, with a crew receiving monthly wages, whereas the smaller schooners were usually owned by one or two men.

The four-masters were lean and sleek, with sharp clipper bows and masts soaring 150 feet above the deck. Their sails reached a hundred feet from boom to gaff, creating a breathtakingly graceful sight when under a full spread of canvas, and just as distinguished as the western ocean packets or the Cape Horn clippers. It was no problem for a square-rigger to run offshore and ride out a gale under topsails, but the schooner's salvation lay in her skipper's ability to anticipate the weather, shorten sail ahead of a storm, run for the lee of an island or bay, and drop anchor.

Zeb undoubtedly considered himself lucky to be hired by one of the most reputable men of his time. Sea captains were heroes in those days, and Zeb not only knew of Josiah Cleveland's accomplishments, but probably was attracted to the more independent way of life associated with smaller vessels. Captain Cleveland knew all the secrets of successful coasting, took advantage of every opportunity and trusted to nothing but his own judgment and the simple gear of the *Eliza Jane.* One mistake, one careless move and he and his schooner might easily be lost. Many a crew caught offshore in raging seas took to the shrouds with only a load of lumber aboard keeping their vessel afloat. But there was plenty of money to be made in coasting and Josiah had proven himself able in this respect as well.

Cleveland's *Eliza Jane* was a trim little two-master, capable of carrying forty tons. She had a main topmast, but unlike most schooners her size, raised only a single jib, a monstrous piece of canvas with reef points for use in heavy weather. She also swung a huge fisherman's staysail when the wind was light. Like most Vineyard schooners, she was a centerboarder, which gave her greater maneuverability in shoal waters. Her little dory, which all coasters towed or hoisted astern, Josiah had built himself with characteristic thrift. He had also done much of the carpentry on the schooner while she was under construction in New Bedford.

35

LEFT: Vineyard Haven Harbor with the paddle steamer *Martha's Vineyard* at the pier. *Collection of the author.* OPPOSITE, ABOVE: A coasting schooner bound for Edgartown seen from the beach at Chappaquiddick. BELOW OPPOSITE: The north shore Harris brick yard at Roaring Brook. *Both courtesy of the Vineyard Gazette*

Able, shrewd, exacting and canny Captain Cleveland knew a good thing when he saw it and he was quick to hire Zeb, who had already earned quite a reputation working in the clay pits during school vacations. There, Zeb's unusual strength and speed enabled him to do the work of two men, and he was paid accordingly. No doubt Cleveland figured he was getting two men for the price of one.

Like all hands signing aboard for the first time, Zeb brought along his own "donkey's breakfast," a mattress filled with hay or straw. While some captains ran seagoing slums with bedbug- and roach-infested cabins, Josiah was as meticulous as an old maid housekeeper; his cabin was immaculate. Zeb learned quickly, however, that Cleveland's exacting nature extended to more than housekeeping.

Shortly after he had signed on, the *Eliza Jane* was tied up alongside the steamboat wharf in Vineyard Haven taking aboard supplies. Ben Franklin Cleveland, Josiah's son and mate, was up-street getting groceries while Zeb refilled the water kegs kept on deck just forward of the cabin. When he stopped for a moment to pull out a splinter, Josiah, who was stowing gear in the lazarette, caught sight of Zeb out of the corner of his eye. The captain could see the boy was about to bunch up his day. "No! No! Young feller! Wait'll Sunday!" he called to his new hand, whose upbringing hadn't been synchronized with clock, sun or tide. Zeb hurried back to work, saving his splinter for the Sabbath.

Josiah had, at one point, contracted to freight a load of small pink brick to Newport from Charles Harris' brick and clay company situated on the Vineyard's north shore. Although little is known about Zeb's early years sailing with Josiah, there is a record of several trips from Charles Harris' own diary. It is this document that supplies much of the detail from which the following account of the voyage—probably a typical one—is drawn.

When they left Vineyard Haven that June morning in 1883, the wind lay in the northeast, dictating the character of the day. Picking up a following sea as she rounded the outer mark in Vineyard Haven Harbor, the *Eliza Jane* moved westward along the north shore. From the vessel one could see small farms and an occasional oak or pine, twisted and bent by the will of the winds sweeping up the coast.

At that time there were five separate brick, paint and clay works nestled alongshore with wharves extending well out into deep water. Towards the western end of the

A fish weir off the north shore in use in the 1940s, much as it was in the 1880s. *Photo: Jan Hahn, courtesy of the Vineyard Gazette.*

north side of the island were the Harris wharves, alongside of which Josiah brought the *Eliza Jane* to hand-load the small pink blocks. It was slow work. Barehanded, Zeb and Ben picked up four or five brick at a time from the wheelbarrows in which they were brought down the pier, and with a slight toss passed them to Josiah in the hold. With customary speed and efficiency, the captain stacked the brick between layers of straw to prevent chipping or breaking. Experienced men had hands tough as shark-skin; gloves wore out too quickly to be anything but a nuisance.

When they had about twenty-five hundred brick stored in the hold for ballast, the northeast winds brought in a squall and heavy seas. Charles Harris reported in his diary, "Squall came from N.NE. Left wharf and cut from mooring. Stood to westward on port tack. Had to 'bout ship to avoid pound (fish weir). Missed stays (failed to come about) and came near drifting into the pound. Then stood to the east by wharf, then on port tack offshore—Time 4 P.M."

Skippers had to react quickly to such hazards. Many southern New England coastal areas were fringed with these weirs which extended a thousand feet or so out from shore. When the storm abated, Josiah moved the *Eliza Jane* back to the wharf and put the balance of the cargo on the schooner's deck with stanchions around the rail to hold it. They had twenty-five tons of brick aboard by nightfall, ready to sail for Newport on the early morning tide.

As the *Eliza Jane* moved up Vineyard Sound, setting a course for Newport, Zeb undoubtedly had plenty to see. The coast was covered with canvas: large and small schooners carried raw materials and produce; packets ran between the competing ports of Boston and New York; fishing smacks, barges and paddle steamers plied the waterways. Clay, pig-iron and silver bar sailed into Taunton, Massachusetts; steamers and schooners fed cotton to the great textile mills of Fall River, whose damp climate was ideal for handling the thread; and sloop-rigged Maine scows supplied southern New England farms with hay and cordwood.

The Swinburne, Peckam establishment in Newport in the 1880s. LEFT: The lumber yard, with brick stacked under the scaffold at right. RIGHT: The front office. *Both, Newport Historical Society.*

With fair sailing, it was a run of several hours from the Harris brick works to the entrance of Narragansett Bay which is interrupted by many small islands. Newport itself is on a large island called Aquidneck, an Indian name meaning Island of Peace. Her tranquil beauty belied a stormy past, buffeted by the Revolution, the War of 1812 and the controversial Triangle Trade. During the latter period, Newport citizens got rich dispatching rum to Africa in exchange for slaves. The slaves were then shipped to Barbados and traded for molasses and sugar to make more Newport rum.

Aquidneck is flanked by an East and a West Passage, the East leading to the Taunton River and the town itself, and the West Passage leading on up the Providence River.

Newport itself has an outer and an inner harbor. Around Cattle Point sailed the *Eliza Jane*, past Fort Adams which protected the inner harbor's entrance, and into the port itself where vessels lay close in on every side waiting to load or unload fruit, tobacco, sugar, stone and lumber. The more than fifty taverns and saloons clustered about gave an immediate indication of the volume of maritime traffic.

Zeb and Ben had little time to sample these attractions, however. It made no difference how quickly they unloaded their cargo, out of habit Captain Cleveland would urge them to hurry along. One wonders how much they were able to see of Newport itself. The old part of town, nestled against the harbor, was distinguished for its stately captains' houses, vine-hung, hip-roofed cottages, narrow, cobbled streets and the historic Trinity Church. The "new" part of town, along Bellevue Avenue, boasted architectural behemoths in English, Italian, French and German styles, monuments to the tastes and ambitions of the giants of the Industrial Revolution.

As soon as the last of the brick went over the caplog, Josiah settled up with the Swinburne Peckham yard, collecting $6.50 per ton for the brick plus $2.00 per ton freightage.

Since there was no profit in running light, Josiah usually managed to acquire 39

ABOVE, LEFT: The Newport of the Vanderbilts; the State Dining Room of "The Breakers." ABOVE RIGHT: Long Wharf in Newport, with fishing boats unloading their catch, which was immediately put into barrels and shipped to Boston and New York. *Rhode Island Collection at Providence Public Library.*

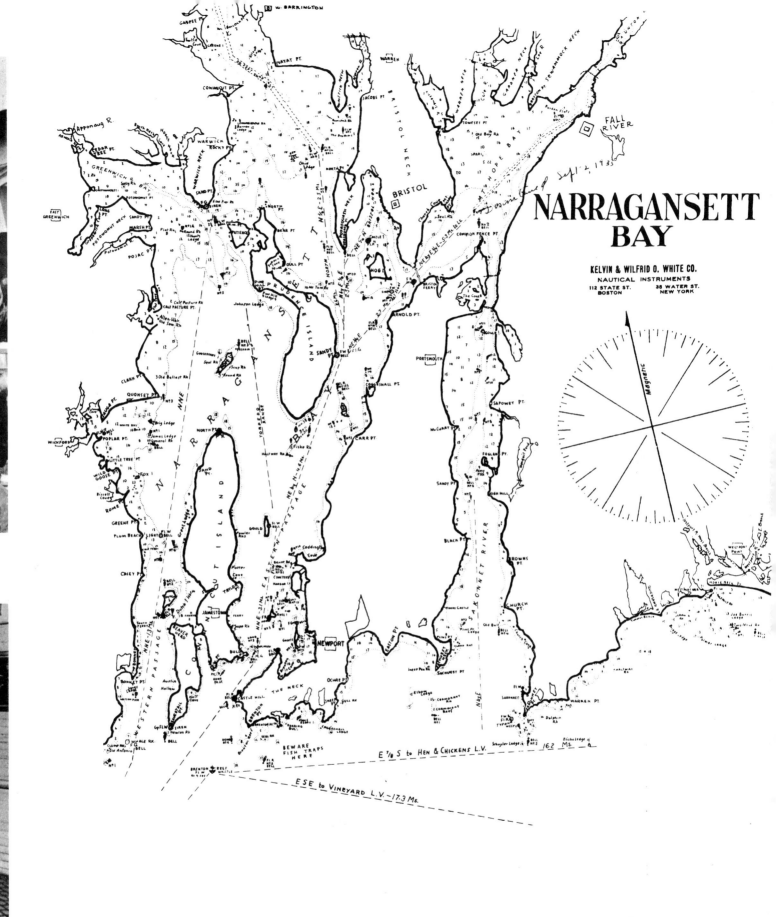

OPPOSITE, LEFT: Long Wharf stacked with cordwood and surrounded by fishing and cargo vessels. *Newport Historical Society.* OPPOSITE, RIGHT: A Long Wharf saloon. *Courtesy of Captain Wilfred Warren, collection of the author.* ABOVE: Detail from the 1920 *Eldridge Tide and Pilot Book.*

another cargo on the mainland before heading home. Several times that summer he had picked up ice in New Bedford bound for the Vineyard's budding resort town, Cottage City. New Bedford may well have been his next port of call on this trip, too.

When it came time to cast off from the Newport dock, Zeb and Ben would go to work raising the mainsail. As they faced each other, each with his hands on the halyard, left close above left, their right hands reached for the next hold above their heads. With perfect coordination, their bodies came down in unison to inch the heavy canvas up the mast.

If the weather was favorable, the topsail was set and clewed up as they sailed down the bay. Into the sound they went, leaving the Hen and Chickens Lightship, midway in the entrance to Buzzards Bay, to starboard.

As they approached New Bedford, the peaceful Acushnet River gave no clue to the importance of the whaling port which was usually jammed with vessels from all over the world. Josiah always came to anchor on the Fairhaven side, off the bank opposite New Bedford. The anchor chain encircled the barrel of the windlass in three round turns and was tiered in a box on deck. The boys would have the chain overhauled and flaked down on deck ahead of the windlass so it ran clear. Jib halyard coils had been taken off the pins and checked to be sure they were clear for lowering. Then Josiah would ease the helm and luff up to anchor. As the *Eliza Jane* rounded into the wind, the boys let the headsheets fly. At a shout from the captain to "Let her go," the anchor splashed. More chain was fed out, and with a final jerk, the vessel acquiesced. The boys dropped the foresail and secured lines. Once a schooner was dead in the wind, however, her heavy sails caused little trouble. In fact, the huge mainsail was sometimes left up on a still night.

After furling sail and coiling halyards, Zeb and Ben hung the big riding lights in the rigging while Josiah went below to cook dinner. The cabin, with its cookstove against the forward bulkhead, bunks lining the sides, table and chairs in the center and a kerosene lamp swinging on gimbals, was probably warm and comfortable.

There was little formality on coasting schooners compared to the carefully ranked crews of the deepwater vessels which spent months or even years at sea. Captain and crew, except on the largest schooners, always shared the same quarters. The food on most coasters was better than on deepwater ships, but Cleveland's Yankee frugality

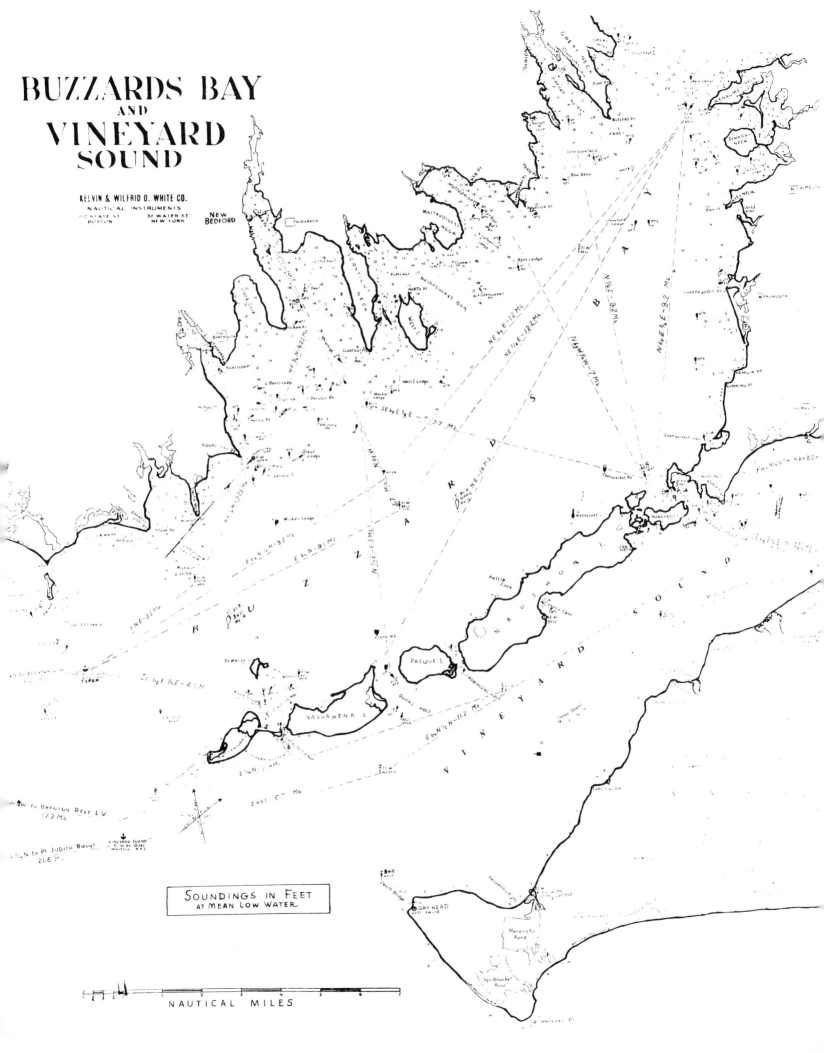

BUZZARDS BAY
AND
VINEYARD
SOUND

KELVIN & WILFRID O. WHITE CO.
NAUTICAL INSTRUMENTS

SOUNDINGS IN FEET
AT MEAN LOW WATER

NAUTICAL MILES

LEFT: A surviving eel pot made by Josiah Cleveland. *Photo: Alfred Eisenstaedt.* OPPOSITE: The horse-drawn trolley taking tourists from the Cottage City pier to the campground. *Photo: Marshall R. Cook Studio.*

extended right down to the galley. Little time was expended cooking or eating. The three men lived on salt herring, cod and hardtack. The old skipper considered anything more a waste of time and money. The herring was kept in a barrel directly below the kerosene lamp where, in rough weather, the lantern fuel would drip on the fish. Josiah forbade anyone to alter this arrangement. "A little kerosene on the fish keeps my men frisky," he boasted, pleased with his nutritional innovation, which probably served likewise to cut down on the herring consumption.

Ship visiting, or wandering around the waterfront, was a common way to end the day for men in the coastal trade, and undoubtedly Zeb was eager to go ashore. He was a restless lad on the brink of manhood and had been accustomed to a casual, unfettered existence on the Vineyard. Josiah, on the other hand, was seldom disposed to leave his schooner unless it was totally necessary. If he made no move to lower the dory, it was out of the question for his crew as well. The old man didn't care much for mainlanders. Instead, he preferred to stay below, weaving oak strips and scrub pine roots together, a performance that must have aroused Zeb's curiosity the first time he saw it. But a new hand on a vessel didn't ask questions—he watched, listened and took orders.

Josiah was, in fact, at work making eel traps—a small enterprise he operated on the side. The handsome beehive-shaped pots were worth six dollars apiece, and Josiah wasn't one to waste time when that kind of money was at stake.

Eeling was a lively business on the island. The pots were placed along the pond shores with weirs fanning out like picket fences which would funnel the big silver eels into the traps as they began their autumn migration back to the Sargasso Sea. Packed alive in barrels, they were then shipped out of Vineyard Haven on the 6 A.M. boat for New Bedford, where they caught the early steamer for profitable sale in New York.

Thus Zeb and Ben often had to content themselves with sitting on deck. If it was a still night, bursts of singing, cursing and shouting would waft across the water from the brightly lit taverns and saloons, mirrored in the calm water of the harbor. The only other sounds might be the periodic bark of a dog alongshore or the slap of halyards against the mast when the schooner answered to the wake of a passing vessel.

Before going to bed, Cleveland always set an empty pan on the stove. One end of a long line was attached to the handle and a weight was tied to the other end. Each night he took the weighted end of the line up the companionway, dropped it off the

stern of the vessel and without a word returned to the cabin, ducking under his ingenious contraption. When the tide changed, the schooner would swing on her chain, causing the pan to hit the floor with a crash, thus signalling time to start loading. The old man's deep and lifelong mistrust of clocks went to the very marrow of his bones. A mess of gears, wires and springs might refuse duty, but the tide never failed.

According to his precise routine, Josiah would leap from his bunk calling, "Hurry, hurry, boys 'fore the day's ruined!" and dash up the companionway to check the weather. The boys were expected to stir the fire to life before Josiah returned to put the big coffee pot on to boil. After washing themselves in a bucket of fresh water from one of the barrels on deck, the boys refilled the bucket and put it on the back of the stove for washing up after breakfast. In no time the smell of wood smoke, coffee and salt cod filled the cabin, and in even less time breakfast was consumed. The dishes were stacked in a pan wedged tightly in a corner, to be washed after they got under way. The boys went back on deck. They rarely needed to pump the *Eliza Jane*, so with the aid of a log windlass and the jib, they broke out the anchor. They would then come alongside the pier, load the ice for Cottage City, and head for the Vineyard with the full benefit of the tide.

Cottage City was proud of its tourist trade in the 1880's, though it was hardly in competition with Newport and didn't wish to be. Cottage City promotions boasted a "cozy sociableness and a most attentive politeness without a single dash of Chesterfield in it. ... We don't want the blacklegs of Newport or those of that character who visit that place in summer; nor do we wish to furnish drinking and smoking saloons to rowdy customers; and we certainly don't want the conceited fop nor the pert miss who have not enough sense for any manly or truly feminine enjoyment."

Originally a campground of tents in an oak grove where outdoor revival meetings were held, the settlement gradually became a summer resort, too, although a seven-foot fence around the thirty-six acres of the Camp Meeting Association safely separated the saintly from the secular. Spawned and nurtured by Methodists, the camp meeting drew ever increasing flocks of church groups from all over the east. The rise of Cottage City as an elegant resort was more irregular, though determined. As land development boomed, schooners rushed in raw materials for the construction of the fashionable cottages, all of which were replete with rococo verandas, high-pitched roofs, gables, 45

OPPOSITE: The *Active* leaving Cottage City for Edgartown. *Photo: Marshall R. Cook Studio.* RIGHT: The paddle steamer *Monohansett*, the small passenger vessel *Helen Augusta*, and what is probably a square-rigged warship in the background. *Photo: Marshall R. Cook Studio.*

turrets, spires, scrollwork along the eaves, leaded arch windows and fancy cut shingles. Nestled close together, some not four feet apart, and often painted in rainbow variety, they formed a setting fit for Hansel and Gretel.

As the *Eliza Jane* and her cargo pulled alongside the Cottage City wharf, Zeb and Ben probably watched—and not without scorn—the tourists and church brethren alighting from the paddle steamer *Monohansett*, some to go to the new Sea View Hotel which advertised speaking tubes in every room and a water view for a dollar a day, others to board a splendid little train pulled by the *Active*, the island's pride and joy. The small locomotive whistled a salute and stood waiting, with her imposing funnel and gleaming cowcatcher ready to lead the way down her narrow-gauge track to Edgartown and out to the magnificent surf at South Beach. The engine's debut some nine years earlier, however, had very nearly never taken place.

The *Active* had been lashed onto a flatcar in the railyard at Woods Hole in 1874, awaiting the paddle steamer voyage across to Martha's Vineyard. Other loaded cars, switched on the same track, lost their brakes, rolled down the rails and struck the *Active's* flatcar, shoving it forward until it hit hard against the caplog. The jolt pitched the *Active* off the flatcar, through the air, and down to the bottom of Woods Hole Harbor. Fished out as quickly as possible, the sturdy machine had sustained only a smashed cowcatcher and acquired a bit of seaweed in her cylinders. Once safely installed on the island, she soon became a landmark with her passenger coach upholstered in red plush, a handsome excursion car and a boxcar, all with lamps at each end.

If Zeb and Ben had ventured ashore they would have seen the vacationers promenading along the boardwalk or whirling around the new roller skating rink where, it was once reliably reported, they skated to the strains of "Nearer My God to Thee." Across the street the Flying Horses revolved young dandies who lunged out for the brass ring as they spun around.

Although disallowed during Camp Meeting Week, croquet madness had gripped the whole community at this time and tourists, ministers and their flocks were at it night and day. The *Vineyard Gazette* claimed the game "tends to softening of the brain," and one righteous critic protested it was "the only development liable to lower the moral standard of the camp and we have yet to witness a game in which cheating

47

LEFT: A wistful wader off the Cottage City beach. BELOW: Croquet at the campground. OPPOSITE, LEFT: Catboats for hire at the pier. *Photos: Marshall R. Cook Studio.* OPPOSITE, RIGHT: The community pump for the use of vacationers at the campground. *Martha's Vineyard Historical Society.*

and lying are not uncommon occurrences, especially among the fair sex. We have seen ministers' daughters do it time and again."

In spite of this unsettling report, schooners freighted in hundreds of croquet and archery sets and the town's reputation for fun and games became secure.

Though men of the schooner trade didn't take vacations, they did entertain themselves at the expense of the tourist. Such visitors were tolerated but not welcomed by the seamen, who eyed them with considerable disdain. One earnest vacationer approached a well-known Cottage City catboat skipper who always wore an old farmer's straw hat to keep the sun off his shiny bald head. The tourist warned the captain, saying, "Don't you realize the reflection from water burns your face?"

"More'n likely," replied the skipper. "But the reflection from the sun'll burn a hull lot more."

As soon as the *Eliza Jane* had been unloaded and Josiah had received payment for the ice, they sailed back to Vineyard Haven where they usually laid in for a few days between trips. Josiah would go up to his house on the West Chop shore to see his family and check on his various enterprises. Among these was the drying of salt herring. To begin the process, salt was added to a barrel of water until it could float a potato. Then more salt was tossed in for good luck, and the fish were added and left to pickle for a week or longer. If the fish were used at home, they were removed from the barrel only when needed. If meant for sale, they were taken out, dried on flakes, packed in dry salt and sent to market in barrels. Herring was sold like licorice at ten cents for a string of them on a stick. Catching the fish was an annual event. In the spring, when the herring swam up the creeks to spawn, one would hear the cry, "They're showering," which brought everyone running to begin the back-breaking job of hauling in the nets.

Like Josiah, Zeb went home between trips, bringing with him whatever money he had managed to save from his ten-dollar-a-month salary. Often he carried home a sack of potatoes or turnips he had bought cheaply from another schooner as a present for his father. If there was time to spare, he worked in the clay pits for a few days, or helped his father cut a supply of wood for the winter.

For entertainment there were weekly Tucker parties in the Chilmark Town Hall on the Middle Road. All the Tilton boys attended; square dances and quadrilles were the evening feature. The girls, dressed in sundowns, gingham, black stockings and high

Leary's log raft and a few of the many who were eager to be photographed aboard it. *Courtesy of the Vineyard Gazette.*

button shoes, came in from the surrounding countryside. Whether it was due to shyness or embarrassment over his crossed eyes, Zeb never danced. At these parties he would hang back and watch, even though he was a fervent admirer of the opposite sex.

During one such visit, when the family was gathered for supper, Zeb noticed his brother John had a black eye. Questioned about it, John explained that a boxing coach and some students from Harvard University were camping out on the north shore. When John had come along, they talked him into a match. Unable to take care of himself as well as the other Tilton boys, he was quickly knocked to the ground.

Zeb listened intently, his crossed eyes drawing in closely towards his nose as he studied his brother. At last he stood up, stretched, and declared that he felt like taking a short walk. Zeb then set out through the woods for the campsite. The boxing coach was delighted to find another untrained country boy he could goad into a match to impress his students. He offered to box with Zeb, who refused. The students then joined in, urging him on, whereupon Zeb agreed with apparent reluctance. His fists quickly found their target. Zeb's reach was enormous, and in short order the boxing coach of Harvard University lay on the ground.

Zeb turned and walked slowly back to the house without saying a word. He picked up his sailor's bag, bid his family good-bye, and started down the road for Vineyard Haven.

It was during Zeb's early years on the *Eliza Jane*, when industry in the northeast was coming to full flower, that an enterprising young Nova Scotian named Leary astounded Vineyarders and other east coast communities with his remarkable log raft. Leary apparently decided that the simplest way to transport timber south was to tie the logs together and tow them, rather than to go to the trouble and expense of shipping them by schooner. Without further ado he built a raft that might have filled nearly forty schooners—made up of 24,000 logs, 592 feet long and valued at $75,000. This well-publicized leviathan plowed into Vineyard Haven Harbor in early August of 1888 to the amazement of crowds who lined the shore to stare or to climb aboard to have their pic-

An osprey nest against the backdrop of Whale Hill on Gardiner's Island. *Photo: Alfred Eisenstaedt.*

tures taken. Its stay in Vineyard Haven was short but spectacular. On August 8, the logs were towed out of the harbor by the steam tugs *Underwriter* and *Ocean King* and headed toward New York.

The mushrooming of industry along the east coast heightened the appetite for raw materials and stimulated the corollary need for delivery of finished products to the marketplace. A log raft was only one example of the ingenuity resulting from such increased pressure. The coastal schooner business prospered under these conditions, especially with such able seamen as those on board the *Eliza Jane*.

Zeb had proved to be an extraordinary foremast hand. He had memorized the coastline, could anticipate the slightest change in weather, and was a match for the heaviest cargo. In spite of his bulk—shoulders like spars and hands that hung to his knees—he was agile as a cat and went aloft with the ease and speed of a man half his size. He once explained that he took after his mother, who was so spry that when she went to bed she could blow out the candle and jump under the quilt before the room got dark.

Though it must have been visibly apparent that coasting came naturally to Zeb, it was eight years before Josiah was convinced. Once assured, however, he began to allow Zeb to skipper the *Eliza Jane* alone, while he attended his businesses on shore. For Josiah, it demonstrated a prodigious faith that no one else could have inspired in him.

In the 1890's Zeb, Ben and Josiah made several trips to Gardiner's Island to pick up clay for the pottery at New London. It was an especially profitable cargo which appealed to Cleveland. For several weeks one summer, they dug the clay out of the cliffs at Whale Hill and carted it down the pier in specially made wheelbarrows. Several days' work was needed just to load the schooner, even with Josiah cracking the whip. He kept the boys at work even if it meant loading by lantern after dark. When Ben complained one evening that the sun had long since set, his father shouted, "Keep on! Keep on! There be another one up soon." Though they did quit eventually that night, they were hard at it again before the next sun appeared. Josiah couldn't bear to see 53

Millstone Point Quarry, from where fine building granite was shipped down the river through New London. Much of this stone was used in the construction of the U.S. Military Academy at West Point. *Courtesy of the New London County Historical Society.*

anyone relax; it was nearly immoral. Even when the boys sat down for lunch of hard-tack and herring, impatience got the better of the old man. He'd smile thinly and bark, "While you're resting boys, throw some more clay in the cart."

They made the short run across Long Island Sound several times that summer. New London was a busy port in the 1890's. The Thames River, on whose bank the city lay, was the artery for the "Brownstone fleet" which freighted building stone from the Waterford and Hartford areas to New York. Passenger steamboats ran daily to New York and, in summer, to Sag Harbor, Greenport, Watch Hill and Block Island.

Industry was growing in New London with machine shops, printing presses and the manufacture of silk goods. It was also an important sealing center where pelts from Labrador were made into coats. The pottery factory which turned out plates, pitchers, mugs and bean pots, depended on the schooners to bring in its raw material.

Although clay was never the cleanest of cargoes, Josiah always managed to keep his schooner in Bristol fashion. When her bottom needed a fresh coat of paint, he'd run her up on the beach and heel her over, first to paint one side at low tide, then the other. Despite such care, she occasionally needed a complete overhaul which involved an expense Josiah tried to delay as long as possible. When the job could wait no longer, the *Eliza Jane* was taken to the shipyard at New Bedford.

Lining the city's Center Street were warehouses in which were stored the casks of fine whale oil used for machinery. Bales of cotton destined for the mills were piled high on the wharves; the fishing fleet jammed the piers on both sides of the harbor; and packet boats were regularly arriving from or departing for the Azores and Cape Verde Islands. As soon as the *Eliza Jane* was pulled up on the railway, Zeb had the rare chance to go to town and see the sights. Half the population was foreign-born and the streets were crowded with Portuguese, French, Scandinavians, British and even exotic Polynesians who had signed aboard at some far-flung South Pacific port.

The Alaskan gold rush had sent many sailors west, smitten with the image of wealth. During this period one of the first seamen's strikes along the ports from Boston to New York took place. Good men were in very short supply. Blood money was high and the crimps who coerced seamen into joining a ship's crew were filling the fo'c's'le with anyone they could find. Tom Codd was the chief crimp at the time, according to

RIGHT: A fleet of coastal schooners at the pier or at anchor in New London Harbor about 1890. BELOW: Two-masted schooners along the Thames River shore in New London undergoing repair work. *Both courtesy of the New London County Historical Society.*

A Canadian lumber schooner, the *Maple Leaf,* headed for New York. *Photo: © Mystic Seaport, Rosenfeld Collection, Mystic, CT.*

James Williams, one of the founders of the American Seamen's Union, and Codd's chief runner was Big Joe Beef. The latter would meet an incoming vessel, entertain the crew with liquor and women, and sell the men off to another vessel at one hundred dollars a head. Or they'd snare wide-eyed boys eager for a taste of what they thought was glorious adventure. While coasters never required such jackal services, any vessel headed on a long voyage depended on them.

Some of the captains frequented the New Bedford Seamen's Bethel, but most sailors headed for Johnny Cake Hill and Water Street where The Spouter Inn, The Harpooner, The Homeward Bound, and other red-light saloons enticed them to part with their pay in a few uproarious hours. Drinking, singing, whoring, bloody battling and callous crimping were regular fare. Although Zeb didn't drink or smoke, the fair sex held special interest for him. New Bedford had more than its share of streetwalkers, "two dollar delights," and tough professionals working with the crimps. For their part, the girls didn't care that Zeb was rough, cross-eyed, or homely. He was witty, virile, fearless and generous to a fault. If a woman pleased him he gave her anything she wanted. Zeb was particularly delighted every time Cleveland put into New Bedford, and so were the girls.

It was inevitable that some female would sooner or later capture this hulking, agreeable man for her own. Doubtless many tried and doubtless it required considerable will power and determination on the part of the easygoing young sailor to resist them.

For all of New Bedford's charms, the first girl to land him came from back home on the Vineyard. Grace Cook, with whom Zeb had been acquainted for some time, was a

Bales of cotton on the New Bedford waterfront, delivered by steamer and schooner, for the booming textile trade that had replaced whaling as the major industry. *Martha's Vineyard Historical Society.*

sultry lass and quite a flirt. They were married in Vineyard Haven in 1894 when he was twenty-eight and Grace nineteen.

Zeb installed his bride in a house up-island near his boyhood home, but Grace never could quite settle down to country living or to being a wife. Zeb, on returning home from a freighting trip, would frequently find her entertaining young men in their house. With Grace shrieking in protest, Zeb would take her over his knee and give her a spanking, though this never effected a change in her behavior. Their marriage lasted only two years.

"She had a diver (different) fancy man every time I put to sea," Zeb explained to a friend lightheartedly. "I think she run off with a diver."

What his true thoughts were about this unfortunate affair, he kept to himself. He never mentioned Grace again.

Single once more (although in truth, married or not, he had regularly practiced the "sailorman's prerogative"), Zeb headed for, among others, a girl he knew in New Bedford. She had continued to pursue him with particular energy, determined never to abandon the hope of marriage as long as he was above ground. Eventually she mustered the courage to broach the subject just as the *Eliza Jane,* her mains'l up and a full load of coal aboard, was ready to cast off.

"Thank you kindly, ma'am, and much obliged. A man can get married any time, but it ain't every afternoon he gets a fair tide and a fair wind for the Vineyard," and he waved her good-bye as they sailed out of the harbor. Zeb had discovered women were easier to acquire than to shake off.

Zeb remained single and sailed from Maine to Connecticut with Josiah for another 57

five years. Their efforts had made the old skipper wealthy. Josiah handled the *Eliza Jane* so skillfully during those years she could almost sail herself. As Zeb explained years later when he was guest speaker at a Barnacle Club Meeting in Vineyard Haven, "We used to lay on the wind when making a passage and secure the wheel with what we called a blind jack—wa'n't nothin' but a stick through the spokes to keep the wheel from turning. Held in this manner in a light, steady breeze, the schooner would hold her course perfectly and we could go about doin' chores without paying any attention to the vessel for long periods.

"Running for Cuttyhunk one day to load paving stones, we secured the wheel and went below to eat dinner. The wind freshened a little, which we failed to notice, and the schooner made the land before we figgered she would. The first thing we knew, a puff of wind struck her and we heard the mains'l slat as she come to. We jumped on deck just in time to see her luff up right in close to the beach. We had fifteen fathom of chain overhauled on deck ready to anchor. As the jib swung inboard, the sheet took a turn around the anchor fluke, lifted it off the rail and dropped it. The vessel settled astern on her cable and laid there just as we intended without a human hand touchin'

Not once in all those years did Zeb's admiration for the old man who taught him all he knew about coasting ever waver. In fact, Cleveland's influence and example set the standard by which Zeb worked for the rest of his life. In his later years he told Joseph Chase Allen of the *Vineyard Gazette*, "I have never seen nor known a man what planned so carefully and perfectly as Josiah. If the wind and tide favored, 'twas never a motion lost. We boated the paving stone off the beach where we picked them up. This was a cargo to sell, wa'n't merely a freight to be earned. The system of handling the stone was so perfect we'd be over the side of the boat as it touched the beach and the stones was goin' aboard at once't. The mains'l was goin' up as the last of the stones went aboard of the schooner and it was goin' up again as the last ones went on the dock. No man who sailed with Josiah could help but learn the rewards of hard work and tending to business."

In spite of Zeb's intense admiration for the old man, he was too wise and able not to realize he could do better for himself. It took a long time to save money when you worked for Cleveland, but by the turn of the century Zeb could finally afford his own vessel, and at thirty-three he was anxious to be off on his own.

LEFT: The Luce grocery store in Vineyard Haven about 1910. *Courtesy of the Vineyard Gazette.* BELOW: The Edgartown office of the *Vineyard Gazette* and the view up North Water Street in about 1900. *Martha's Vineyard Historical Society.*

ZEB AND THE *WILFRED J. FULLER*

As the twentieth century loomed, the *New York Times* boasted that nineteenth-century inventions — steam engines, railroads, the telegraph, ocean liners, electric lights, even the telephone—would soon be surpassed by bigger and better things. "We step on the threshold of 1900 which leads to the new century facing a still brighter dawn of civilization."

The *Vineyard Gazette*, however, wasn't at all concerned with the calendar. Its last issue of the nineteenth century carried the same old ads on the front page along with the usual little anecdotes, while the second page reported that a coal schooner was aground on the Edgartown Harbor side of Cape Pogue and that the schooner *Glide* was busy lightering her. The Chadwick-Dunham assault case over a pile of wood ashes was said to have been amicably settled at a hearing in the Town Hall which was largely attended. There was an article on the Arctic mosquito, and a brief note that cotton mill wages would be going up, while the price for Ideal Windmills remained, as it had for some years, at seventy dollars.

In spite of its reactionary stance in other respects, the Vineyard boasted its own telephone system by 1900, built by a particularly ingenious local physician, Dr. F.C. Lane. It operated from a switchboard in Vineyard Haven and ran to Oak Bluffs and up-island to Gay Head. Because the telephone company on the mainland had refused to install telephones up-island, on the grounds that there would not be enough business to warrant the cost, Dr. Lane decided to take care of the matter himself.

While tinkering with his wires, Dr. Lane, in frock coat and plug hat, was frequently sighted atop a telephone pole looking much like a giant crow. His task completed, the doctor would shinny down with all the poise befitting a man of his profession, mount his horse-drawn buggy, and trot off to tend a patient.

At first the telephone provoked mixed reactions. In the case of Zeb's sister-in-law, who lived near the Tilton farm, a certain confusion was evident. The near-sighted housewife stood in her yard one morning with an armful of wet laundry and a mouthful of clothespins, groping for the clothesline which was out of reach. She made several stabs and missed. "Fred!" she shouted towards the kitchen door, spitting out the pins at the same time, "You put this clothesline too high. I can't reach it!"

"Good Lord!" George Fred Tilton cried, rushing out the back door, "that's the telephone wire, Lucy! Don't you dare to hang clothes to it. Why, they'd be in Edgartown in fifteen minutes!"

"Well," she snapped, "they ought to warn people! Anyone can make a mistake."

Zeb himself had started the new century by buying an ancient Vineyard Haven two-master, the *Wilfred J. Fuller*. She was a hard old hulk with two barnacles for every fastening. Of sixty-ton burden, the *Fuller* had a powerful windlass and an unusually spacious cabin, a "carven" bowsprit (three-sided instead of round), and carried three jibs. Most important to Zeb, she was fast and able in spite of her age.

Completely independent at last, he stood at the helm of his own schooner with that unconcerned manner which had come to inspire confidence in his associates and uncertainty in the females who plotted his capture. He would chatter away to the old *Fuller* by the hour, patting her wheel when she did well, and scolding her when she failed to react as quickly as he wanted.

He never bothered with a chart but had, instead, memorized the location of every ledge and shoal during his years with Cleveland. With such a memory he depended only on a compass, some wind for his canvas, and if he got in a jam, a lead line. This instrument was simply a cylindrical piece of lead, cupped at one end with an eye on the other to attach to a line. When it was dropped overboard and sank to the bottom, Zeb could both measure the water's depth and verify his location by the color and quality of the sand or mud which he found in the cup after it was retrieved. Zeb often said that he knew the color of the bottom all the way from Boston to Brooklyn.

Zeb not only began the new century with his own schooner, he also got himself a new wife. Earthy and sensitive, he had courted girls in every port, and expressed boundless appreciation for "favors" received from either "daughters of joy" or talented amateurs. In Zeb Tilton's view, women were gifts, a pleasure and a sport to be appreciated to the utmost. Not much to look at, he was the answer to many a maiden's prayer, nonetheless. The urge to domesticate this Paul Bunyan of the sea was clearly irresistible.

Still, he avoided a second capture until Edith Mayhew came into his life. A Vineyard girl, she was descended from the Mayhews who had settled the island in 1642. The Vineyard abounded with both Mayhews and Tiltons, and theirs was considered a grand marriage. Zeb, Edith and the two founding families were united in Cottage City in 1901. The bridal pair spent their honeymoon freighting, and then settled down in an up-island house near Zeb's childhood home in Chilmark.

The winter beach at Gay Head. *Photo: Katherine W. Tweed, courtesy of the Vineyard Gazette.*

Their future seemed boundlessly rosy, for, with his fast-growing reputation, Zeb had no trouble getting all the business he could handle. He was unusually hard-working. He was strong, had a natural "feel" for coasting, and required almost no sleep. When they sailed at night, his mate would seldom spell him at the wheel. Even when he did, Zeb would go below for only a short rest. He would lay his pants on the floor beside his bunk, tucked into the top of his high black boots, and keep one ear tuned to the deck. At the slightest irregular sound, Zeb would leap up, be inside his pants and on the deck in seconds.

Zeb ran the *Wilfred J. Fuller* very much as Josiah had the *Eliza Jane*, with one grand exception. After eighteen years of hardtack and herring, Zeb threw all such frugality to the winds. His galley was a gourmet's delight, featuring bread pudding, chowder, gingerbread, and his own specialty, Tilton's Glory, a sort of potato bargain made like a stew, with salt pork, onions, potatoes and hardtack, which perpetually simmered on the back of his stove. His other specialty was Saleratus biscuits, which never failed to rise, but which came in different colors. When he was freighting coal, Zeb never bothered to get the dust off his hands and the biscuits came out of the oven a soft grey. When he freighted bricks, the biscuits were pink.

Josiah's attitude about money had no influence on Zeb either. He spent cash as freely as Josiah had hoarded it and became known as the easiest touch around. Zeb believed money was to be used for life's pleasures and not stowed away like ballast.

In the wintertime, as he had often done with Cleveland, Zeb collected smooth round stones from the beach at Cuttyhunk, from the Vineyard's north shore, and from Chappaquiddick Island to cobble the streets of New Bedford and Providence. Cold weather was ideal for this operation for a very practical reason. "I only go for rock in the winter," he told his brother Willard, "'cause when you get aholt of one you get aholt of a bundle. Saves time." With his bare hands, he'd pick up three or four twenty-pound rocks frozen together on the beach, put them in a specially reinforced dory, and row out to the schooner anchored off the beach. If he was lucky it might be one of those still, cold winter days which made loading a far simpler task. Usually, however, the hours of daylight were too short, with the sky drained of color and the brown landscape bleak and deserted. More often than not, bitter winds swept across the water while the dory bobbed in the choppy, grey-green seas. The weather notwithstanding, Zeb

64

A fishing schooner in winter at the Edgartown wharf. *Martha's Vineyard Historical Society.*

worked comfortably on the beach dressed in a light jacket whose sleeves were always too short for his arms, a felt hat, and tall, size 14 black boots. It was often long after dark before he had a full load aboard.

Getting up sail in winter could be equally strenuous. Frequently the rigging froze and Zeb or his mate would have to go aloft with a wooden mallet to pound the ice off the halyards so they'd run through the blocks. The foresail along the foot also froze when underway, particularly if the sails were old, making it almost impossible to reef down.

Coal was another common cargo for the *Fuller,* though loading and unloading it sometimes required the assistance of an extra hand. With one such load going from New Bedford to Edgartown, Willard talked Zeb into bringing a particular boy on board to help. Zeb looked him over very carefully, and with the instincts that served him well all his life, knew the young man wouldn't amount to much. Still, Willard insisted that the lad would do. They began shovelling the coal into large, specially made buckets, and with the aid of a gaff and a block and tackle, the dray would swing the buckets ashore onto the coal wharf. At once it was evident that the boy wasn't doing his share.

"Laziest feller I ever seen. Clumsy too," Zeb grumbled.

"Oh, I think he be active," Willard tried to reassure him. Just then the boy stumbled on deck and fell headfirst into the hold, but managed somehow to land on his feet.

"See, I told you he be active," Willard smiled, pleased with his judgment.

But Zeb was far from convinced. "Yus," he grumbled in disgust as he threw another shovelful of coal in the bucket, "but only when he's working for himself."

The boy was quickly dismissed when they got back to Vineyard Haven. Another island lad looking for work asked George Fred Tilton for a job. "Why don't you go see my brother Zeb," George Fred suggested. In no time the lad returned and George Fred asked him if he'd gotten the job.

"I didn't even ask," the lad replied. "When I saw him heaving up the mainsail alone, I figgered I wa'n't want to work for anybody what considered that a one-man job."

In addition to hauling freight, Zeb sometimes worked as an anchor dragger—a kind of nautical junkman who combed the surface and scraped the bottom of the sea for flotsam and jetsam. It was a profitable sideline for a man who knew the treacherous shoals of Vineyard Sound where many another less wise captain had lost his ship.

Between 1900 and 1906, sixteen ships were wrecked in Vineyard Sound alone; hundreds had been lost in prior years and their remains were fair game for any salvager. With grappling hooks, blocks and tackle, and his bare hands, Zeb brought aboard abandoned anchors, brass work, chains, wire cables and timber from the wrecks as well as whatever might be left of their cargoes. All this could be sold to New Bedford scrap dealers.

That few could keep up with Zeb's standards and prowess was a measure of his great capacity for work as well as the amount of work there was to do. Martha's Vineyard was humming with activity. Although whalers had disappeared by 1900, West Indian packets and fishing boats still put in to Edgartown and so did the paddle steamer which ran to New Bedford. Streetwalkers appeared when the fleet was in, two billiard and pool parlors flourished, several taverns catered to the sailors who could afford a week's lodging for $1.40, and Blind Dan, the Town Crier, wandered the streets dispensing news for those unwilling to pay the price of a year's subscription to the *Vineyard Gazette*.

Edgartown was a rising summer resort; schooner yachts filled the harbor and cat-

Edgartown in 1900, including the barbershop (LEFT); Blind Dan, the town crier (ABOVE); and Jimmy Yates in his Chappaquiddick ferry. The photograph of Manuel Swartz (RIGHT) was taken by Alfred Eisenstaedt in 1952 in Swartz's famous boatshop. *All courtesy of the Vineyard Gazette.*

boats dodged about taking tourists from the hotels to the bathing beach at Chappaquiddick. Along the waterfront were fishermen's shanties, a fish-packing plant and a general store—a comfortable place smelling of coffee, tarred fishing tackle, oilskin clothing and new leather. Though off-islanders frequented the general store, they did not scare off the regulars who hung around the pot-bellied stove to comment on the news as faithfully as the rise and fall of the tide. They also picked up gossip at the village blacksmith's, or at Manuel Swartz's boat shop where the proprietor turned out his famous catboats. Manuel's renowned workshop was seldom cleaned—it was a diary of shavings, lumber scraps, braces and blueprints.

The bustling scene was a sure indication of changing times, a situation the versatile schooner captain faced with ease. Although the *Maritime Register* reported, as early as 1881, "from the present appearances, the great bulk of coastwise trade will be under the control of steam in another decade," it underestimated the rugged schooners and their masters who, despite such dire predictions, continued to hold their own in the three-way struggle of rail, sail and steam for the control of the freight market.

In the summer of 1906, on a trip down east to pick up a load of cedar fence posts, 67

Zeb had his first fateful encounter with the *Alice S. Wentworth*. He had just put in to Portland Harbor when the sleek two-master shot by him in a good working breeze. Zeb's crossed eyes absorbed every detail. Since few vessels of that size were able to pass any craft with Zeb at the helm, he paid close attention. He watched her clean wake—not a bit of water dragged behind. He eyed her broad waist fit to hold a good-sized cargo and admired her clipper bow. As soon as he came to anchor and furled sail, Zeb pulled up the dory and rowed over to take a closer look at the rival schooner. Seventy-three feet long with a sharp sheer and broad beam—she was a bricker—built to carry 5500 brick on deck. She drew only 5½ feet of water when light and 7½ when fully loaded with a hundred tons. With the centerboard down, she drew seven feet more.

Her cabin was spacious and beautifully paneled from the deckline up, with two bunks on each side and lockers beneath. A large black cookstove sat amidships against the fore cabin bulkhead. Against the aft end of the cabin was a good-sized table and above that a lamp and a shelf for the compass. There was a hole over the compass in the after bulkhead with a sliding panel to cover it when not in use by the man at the wheel.

The schooner, originally called the *Lizzie A. Tolles,* had been built in Norwalk, Connecticut, in 1863 for freighting between Hudson River ports, New York City and Long Island. Her home port was Bridgeport, Connecticut, until 1891 when she was sold down east to Captain Charles Stevens and his brother Arthur. For thirteen years she had sailed in Maine waters freighting coal, lumber and salt. Then in 1904, when she was forty years old, the captain had her rebuilt from stem to stern. She earned a new documentation and was re-christened the *Alice S. Wentworth,* after Captain Stevens' favorite niece.

Zeb had never seen anything he liked better. Her bottom was painted copper red and she was dark green from her waterline to just above the scuppers. There was a handsome spread eagle across her stern. From there to her railcap she was painted black, with two yellow stripes running her length. A couple of hand pumps were just fore of the cabin, with a heavy box built around them to protect them from coal or other bulk cargo. Enthralled, Zeb discussed her attributes with Captain Stevens until well into the evening.

The next morning on the early turn of the tide, Zeb left for Lincolnville to take   69

aboard the fence posts, and sailed on back to the Vineyard with the *Wentworth* on his mind. There she clung for a couple of years until Zeb learned the owner had decided to hire a captain and was searching for just the right man. In spite of his admiration for the *Wentworth,* Zeb was torn. To give up his own schooner meant the loss of hard-won independence, something he did not take lightly. But the *Wentworth* had captured his heart. As far as he was concerned, she was the very best and he had to have her. With no other reason needed, he sold the *Fuller* and took command of the swiftest, handsomest schooner he'd ever seen.

His job was to freight coal from Taunton, Massachusetts, down east to Maine. There, the coast was white with canvas. Lime, boxboard, lumber, pulpwood, granite blocks, potatoes, salted fish and ice were moving south to Boston and points beyond daily.

The *Alice S. Wentworth* lived up to Zeb's expectations in every way, but sailing down east in winter was something of a disappointment. Schooners would get frozen in for weeks at a time and in some areas it was often March before the ice broke. Even in winter, however, the Kennebec River was a beehive of activity despite the fact that no vessels were moving. Freighting ice from Maine was big business in those days. After being cut from the river, it was poled to shore where a long ramp sloped into the water. The ice cakes were sheered smooth by hand and pushed up the ramp into an ice house where they were packed with layers of sawdust from nearby lumber mills. The ice trade had been going on for a century or more. It was in 1805 that Frederic Tudor conceived the novel idea of sending ice to the West Indies. In the next thirty years he made a fortune. Ice was shipped to England and even to New Zealand. The famous British landscape architect A. J. Dowling reported in 1853, "American ice has sent into positive ecstacies all those of the great metropolis (London) who depend upon their throats for sensations."

When spring came and the Kennebec thawed, the schooner fleet moved up to the ice houses. Once loaded, they scattered on a favoring breeze to London, New York, the West Indies and points south; a grand sight sailing down the river in single file.

This kind of work, however, hardly suited Zeb's restless disposition. The endless delays waiting for warm weather seemed the antithesis of all Cleveland had taught him. There weren't even the diversions one could find in Portland and Rockland, well-known for their "lights of love," to divert a coasterman after a hard sail. Zeb would hang around the general store, watching the men cut ice—and even hope the vessel leaked a bit so he could pump her.

Moreover, the delays precluded spending much time on the Vineyard, although Zeb had been home long enough to father two daughters; Rosalie was born in 1904 and Gertrude the following year. The desire to own the vessel he sailed undoubtedly contributed to his decision. So with much reluctance, but true to character, he came to a swift conclusion and parted with the *Wentworth* after two years, giving his brother the unlikely reason, "The owner wanted me to sail up a river so crooked we passed the same barn three times on the way. I couldn't stand it no how and had to give her up."

He had had the opportunity to repurchase the *Fuller* and he again went back to freighting for himself. But now that he had sailed the *Wentworth,* held her wheel, felt her catch any vagrant breeze when she had her big mainsail, both topsails and fisherman set, with jibs arched to the wind, nothing would ever be the same again. John Leavitt, seaman on coasters, author, artist and Curator at Mystic Seaport, who sailed on the *Wentworth* some years later, said, "I suppose every man (or boy) who ever went to sea had a favorite vessel. Mine was the handsome *Alice S. Wentworth*.... For a coaster she was fast, and it is safe to say that in her prime she was one of the smartest vessels of her size along the coast. Certainly nothing in her class ever passed her while I knew her."

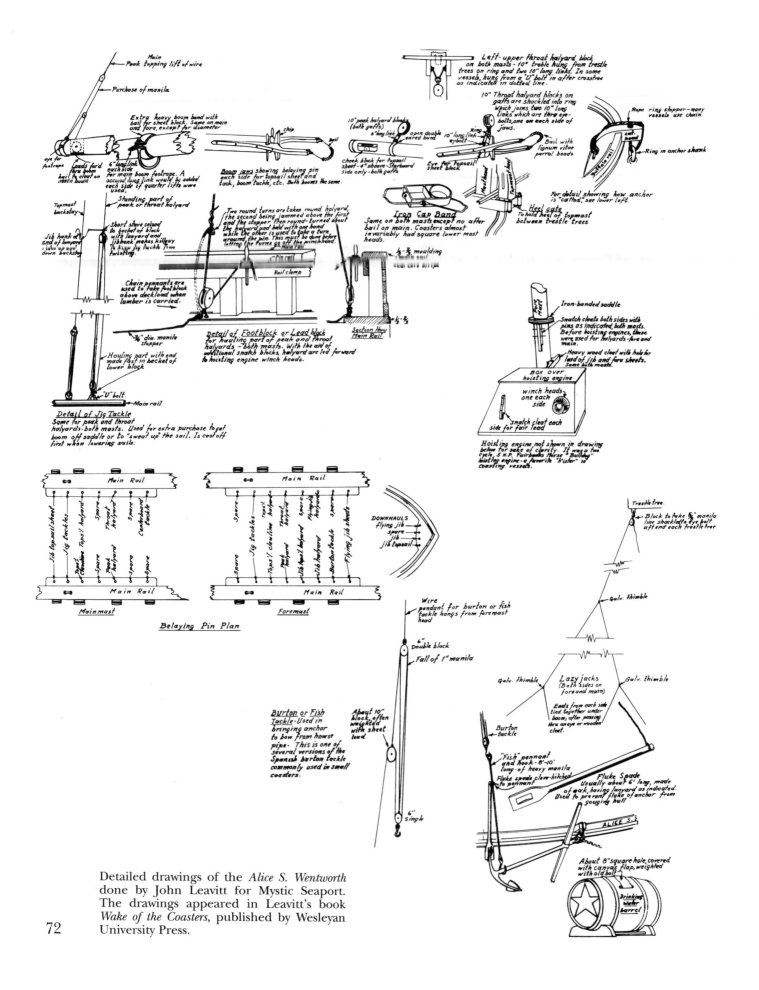

Detailed drawings of the *Alice S. Wentworth* done by John Leavitt for Mystic Seaport. The drawings appeared in Leavitt's book *Wake of the Coasters*, published by Wesleyan University Press.

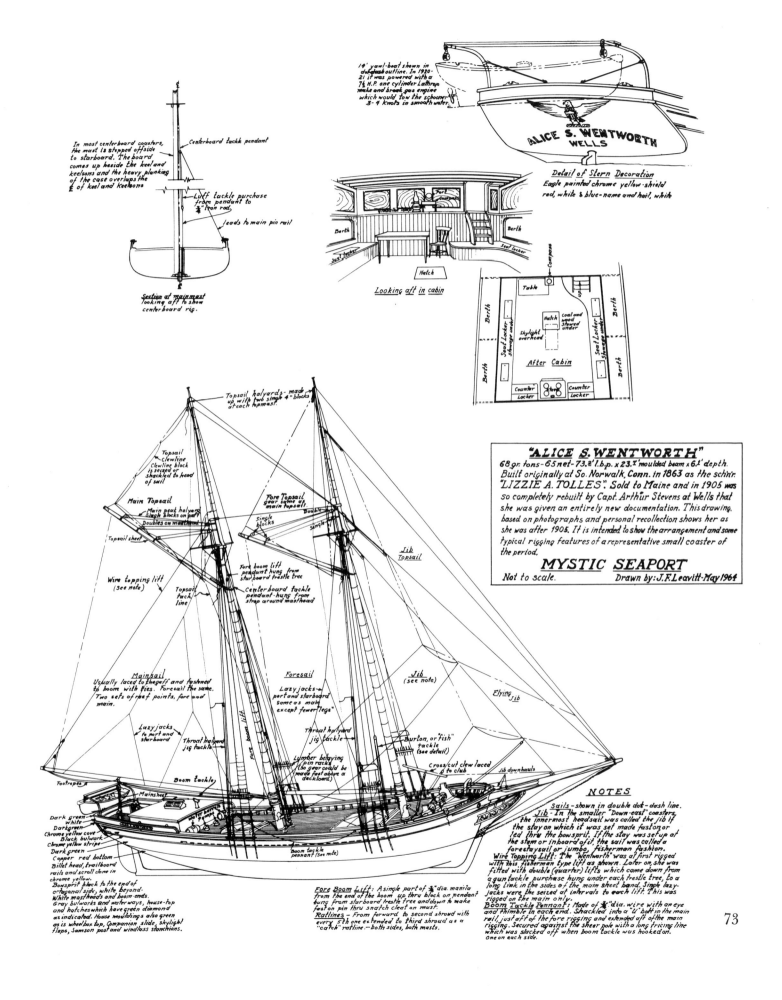

OPPOSITE, TOP LEFT: Sightseers at the Fresnel lighthouse at the top of Gay Head with the oxcart taxi that brought them up from the steamer landing below. *Photo: Baldwin Coolidge, Martha's Vineyard Historical Society.* OPPOSITE TOP RIGHT: A view down the clay cliffs on Gay Head. *Photo: Christopher Harris.* BELOW: Tourists coming ashore at the Gay Head landing below the cliffs. *Courtesy of the Vineyard Gazette.* RIGHT: Gay Head Indians digging clay, which they used for their own pottery or shipped by schooner to the mainland. *Martha's Vineyard Historical Society.*

Still Zeb continued freighting and salvaging in the *Fuller*. He felt at home in the waters of southern New England. Carrying clay to Providence from Gay Head was better than navigating narrow ice-bound rivers in Maine. He would anchor under the familiar, towering cliffs which rose 170 feet above the sea. These spectacular layers of grey, white, yellow, red and black clay exposed by wind and wave, were topped by an extraordinary lighthouse, the work of Augustin Jean Fresnel. Over a thousand prisms, revolving by clockwork, went into this masterful production, which was a renowned attraction for summer tourists.

Paddle steamers from Cottage City, Providence and New Bedford—even Boston and Connecticut—pulled up at the wharf below the cliffs. Ladies gently lifted their skirts to climb into the ox-cart taxis which took them to the top, where shore dinners were served for fifty cents in the Wide Awake Inn and a brass band serenaded the tourists.

Among his friends Zeb counted many Gay Head Indians. This remarkable tribe had earned considerable renown, even before Zeb's time, on whaleships. One member had even attended Harvard as early as 1665 and another served in the state legislature in 1888. They are all immortalized through the character of Tashtego in Herman Melville's *Moby Dick*.

The clay which Zeb freighted had to be dug out of the cliffs and hauled down to the beach by ox cart. Usually a couple of Zeb's Indian friends would give him a hand. With a full load aboard and headed for Providence, the *Fuller* would move past Cutty-hunk Island, leave Sow and Pigs Lightship to starboard as she crossed the southern tip of Buzzards Bay, and beat up the West Passage of Narragansett Bay. Beating up any river fully laden could be a long, exhausting process. The sails would no sooner be filled away than the skipper would call out, "ready about." For a few moments there would be a wild flogging of canvas and loose gear as the vessel came into the end of the wind. As the schooner payed off on the other tack, it was a fast job to get the big headsail flattened in and drawing. There would be just enough time to get the gear coiled down and made ready before it was time to tack again.

Reaching the bridge separating Providence from East Providence, the river narrowed and the wind would often flatten suddenly. Most schooners, if they had a slack or foul tide and no wind, anchored and waited, or else they "kedged up," dropping the anchor forward from the dory and pulling the vessel up to it. Not Zeb. Whenever the

OPPOSITE: The *Henrietta A. Whitney,* a three-masted general cargo schooner whose home port was Ellsworth, Maine. *Photo: © Mystic Seaport, Rosenfeld Collection, Mystic, CT.* RIGHT: The Providence River from the Crawford Street Bridge with schooners tied up on both sides. Rhode Island ca. 1855–1868. *Courtesy of the Rhode Island Historical Society.*

breeze dropped coming into Providence, the mate took the wheel while Zeb jumped into the dory, brought it up to the bow and tied on. Wrapping his enormous hands around his "ash breeze" and bracing his feet, Zeb would bend forward and the oars would bite into the water. The schooner would at first slip back down the river, then gradually come to a halt as the oars bit into the water again and again. Slowly the *Fuller* would begin to move forward towards the clay factory pier. At the right moment Zeb would let up on the oars, the schooner would lose headway and slide up alongside the pier while the mate either tossed a line to someone on the wharf or jumped off and secured it himself.

They would unload until dark, eat supper, and then go ashore to stroll about the waterfront, commenting on the vessels which were tied up and the women who were loose. Providence, the second largest city in New England, was served by railway as well as steamboat lines to Newport, New York, Philadelphia, Baltimore and Norfolk. Her street names—Pound, Sovereign, Shilling, Doubloon, as well as Benefit, Hope and Friendship—reflected her maritime importance in earlier years and her Quaker heritage.

Oil, sugar and salt shipped in from Turks Island and fruits came from all over the West Indies. Rubber, cotton, silver bar and metals arrived to feed the large manufacturing plants which, in turn, shipped out worsted goods, malt liquors, cotton cloth and gold, silver and bronze works of art from the Gorham factory. Brick, boxboard, cement, clay for her pottery and stove-lining factory and other raw materials were brought in by the smaller schooners. The commercial needs of Providence were not unique. In almost all of the ports Zeb visited, heavy loads were moving in and out, day and night, in every season.

Zeb and the *Fuller* never stopped. With an abundance of goods and material to move, the skipper could never rest, though it is doubtful that such an idea ever occurred to him. The strain, however, was greater upon the schooner then upon her captain. The *Fuller* was slowing down. Misshapen from years of heavy freighting, she could no longer meet Zeb's rigorous schedule. The practicalities of earning a living had to take precedence over his obvious sentimental attachment to any vessel and it was undeniable that the *Fuller's* days of freighting for Zeb were over.

LEFT: The *John B. Norris. Peabody Essex Museum.* BELOW: The New York Yacht Club fleet easing in towards Vineyard Haven about 1930. *Photo: A.B. Merry.*

ZEB AND THE *JOHN B. NORRIS*

Zeb had his eye on another old two-master, the *John B. Norris*. He'd once seen her slip through the famous cruising fleet of the New York Yacht Club, which lay on the oily mid-summer waters of Vineyard Sound, drifting with the tide. Eventually the wind had come up, the balloon jibs and spinnakers were broken out and the fleet had begun to move. The captain of the old schooner had no light sails beyond a little gaff topsail and his fisherman's staysail. But, for a coaster, the conditions were perfect—the *Norris* was light, the wind was fair, and with the centerboard raised she had a distinct advantage, as did the skipper, who knew the tricky local currents well. He hung out all his canvas and the *Norris* sailed right through the fleet, leaving the yachts hull-down astern.

The *Norris* could carry sixty tons. She had a broad, low stern, bluff bow, startlingly tall lower masts, narrow-headed sails and had been rebuilt from keel to railcaps. Though she was as old or older than the *Eliza Jane* and the *Fuller*, Zeb figured she'd do. Though the exact date is unknown, the purchase was probably made in 1913 or 1914.

Zeb and the *Norris* had no trouble getting contracts—his reputation for dependability in the coasting trade had spread like a flood tide the length of the New England coast. Manuel Sylvia served as mate and, just as Cleveland had taught Zeb in the years before, now Zeb taught Manuel. The lad's willing struggle to try to keep up with Zeb reflected his admiration; it was a case of hero worship.

Whenever the two of them were under way, Zeb stood at the wheel, his bowed legs giving him sure balance when rolling in a swell. Often he'd be singing "Granny's Old Arm Chair" softly to himself. With a fair breeze, the *Norris* could cut through the water at a steady eight knots—she seemed to know what Zeb wanted of her and he always seemed to anticipate what lay ahead. If they were caught coming down Vineyard Sound in fog so dense Zeb couldn't see the bowsprit from the wheel, he sailed by dead reckoning. Still, in order to check their location, he'd tell Manuel to sniff the air. Smells sharpen in fog, and if Manuel caught a whiff of skunk, Zeb would know they were too close in to Falmouth, on the mainland. But if Manuel's nostrils caught the sweet scent of pine and wild roses, Zeb knew they were on course to leeward of West Chop.

There were other tricks to outwit the fog. "Don't worry none," Zeb would reassure Manuel, "I'll just scoop up some water and taste of it and I can tell where we are. 79

Vineyard Sound, Nantucket Sound and Long Island Sound all taste different." Manuel doubtless eyed his skipper in silence and wonder.

On one occasion, while navigating through the Nantucket shoals, a fog began to roll in, until, as Zeb often said, you could lean on it, or cut it and stack it on deck. The wind dropped and the sails hung flat. Heavy dew dripped from the rigging and the smell of salt and wet raw lumber clung to the deck. Only the ripple of canvas in a brief puff of air, the occasional rattle of a mast hoop and the swirl of water around the rudder interrupted the mournful moan of the fog horn.

Manuel posted himself forward with the lead line and the horn, this time certain they'd run aground, or hit another vessel which could loom up too suddenly to avoid a collision.

"If you see anything, holler," Zeb called to Manuel.

They had ghosted along for only a few minutes when Manuel urgently shouted aft, "Ducks ahead, Zeb!"

"Be they walkin' or swimmin'?"

"Walkin' Zeb, walkin'!" the lad cried in alarm.

"Hard a lee," Zeb called and spun the wheel just as they felt the bottom. Manuel trimmed the jibs while the skipper finished the last verse of his favorite song. Zeb always claimed he could spin the *Norris* around like a button on a backhouse door.

Another extraordinary sailor on the Vineyard was Joshua Slocum, who had settled in West Tisbury around 1906 after his celebrated solitary voyage around the world. The well traveled whalemen on the island thought little of that accomplishment, though to Zeb, who knew Slocum and sometimes went out alone himself, it was an achievement to be admired and respected.

Slocum was a quiet, withdrawn man and always walked with his head lowered. When asked why he had chosen West Tisbury, he said, "It was the dates on the gravestones; by them I concluded that this was about as healthy a place as I could find." He never spoke of his voyages much, but did once tell Zeb about the time he anchored his vessel off a small Pacific island. Some "savages" paddled out in their dugouts, asking for matches. Being a cautious man, Slocum put them in the muzzle of his loaded gun and allowed the natives to pick them out.

Zeb spent little time ashore and at home those years. Nevertheless, he and Edith 81

produced seven more children. In addition to Rosalie and Gertrude, Ruth was born in 1907, Herbert 1909, Alfred 1910, Everett 1912, and Harold 1913. Eight months after Harold, twins were born, but died at birth. When he wanted sleep, Zeb was out of luck at home. He told his wife to slosh buckets of water against the house all night so it would sound like the sea slapping against his schooner. Understandably she refused, leaving Zeb no choice but to walk back to the harbor to get a good night's rest.

He brought Edith what money he had, if someone else hadn't gotten it before he reached home, which was not uncommon since he was still well known as the easiest touch in New England. His favorite presents for the children were bean pots from the Somerset or Providence pottery. This did not seem to diminish their fondness for him any more than his insistence that they have more schooling than he had had. Rosalie, the oldest, adored her father and their similar personalities insured a life-long bond. She seemed to live only for the moment he came trudging up the road and would always be the first to race down to greet him. After supper she'd curl up in his lap and twist her hands around his suspenders so he wouldn't get away. But more often than not, she'd waken in the morning to discover he'd left on the turn of the tide.

There were older girls all along the coast who also wanted to keep their hands wrapped around his suspenders, but they had no more success than Rosalie. Time was money in coasting, as Cleveland had taught, and there wasn't a moment to be lost.

By 1906, steam had overtaken sail running south from New York, contrary to the situation in New England waters. Sail tonnage there was at its peak in 1909, although shipments made by rail, steam and barge were increasing. The old ways would not last forever.

The Vineyard had been making the change from a whaling and farming community to a resort and commercial fishing center, with Vineyard Haven the business hub of the island. An increasing number of boatyards there began to supply gasoline engines. Contractors, carpenters and plumbers advertised the new Eddy Ice Refrigerator, the most up-to-date coal furnaces and sanitary plumbing.

Cottage City, or Oak Bluffs as it was now called, was in its prime, boasting the completion of the Tivoli Casino where, for a nickel, one danced the horse trot—a sort of loping cakewalk with the girl going backwards. Hotels and boarding houses had sprung up to meet the tourist demand. Off-island orchestras and player pianos rang out

with *In the Good Old Summertime, I want a Girl, Meet Me in St. Louis, Louis* and *Bye, Bye Blackbird.* Joy's Pier offered its fleet of party catboats for water-borne tourists as well as electric cars for those needing overland transport. But Edgartown was vigorously challenging Oak Bluffs as a summer resort, and to a lesser degree so was West Chop, which was having its own land-development boom.

The small schooners continued to freight what steamboats couldn't get between decks; often odd cargoes, special orders, and considerable regular loads of fish and ice. The number of coal- and lumber-laden schooners sailing through Vineyard Sound daily was still impressive. Clay, stone and cranberries were still being exported, and many of the island's youth still went to sea.

Coasting remained a risky trade and totally unsuited for the weak or dull-witted. Zeb, who never fit either description, sailed into Menemsha one late summer's day in 1909 to pick up a cargo of barreled salt herring for New York. Jack Jenkinson, who lived in Chilmark and also occasionally mated for Zeb on the *Norris,* was aboard this particular trip and recalls a near disaster. No sooner had they pulled up at the wharf than Zeb, who had an eye like an osprey for weather, saw thick black clouds come over the horizon with a look of wind under them. He and Jack hove to out in the Bight, put the barrels below, battened down the hatches and dropped both anchors.

As Zeb had guessed, the winds rose to gale force and then to hurricane strength, screaming across the sound, tearing and whipping the sea into an angry froth. The *Norris* tossed around on her chain like a bobbing cork. The sea suddenly flattened to a dead calm as the eye of the storm passed, the wind hauled, then shrieked across the Bight again from the other direction strong enough to blow the hair off a dog. The schooner swung on her chains and this time began to drag anchors. The swollen seas and surging current took her right up Menemsha Creek and into Menemsha Pond.

"Weren't such a bad breeze," Zeb explained to Donald Poole, who was later to become one of the island's most famous fishermen. "Why, we was carried right up into that farmer's garden where we could pick all the vegetables we wanted." When the "breeze" had died out, Zeb simply jumped into the dory and towed the *Norris* out of the creek, and they made sail for New York.

Between New York and Boston, the navigational hazards were plentiful in spite of many new buoys, beacons and lighthouses that had been installed since Zeb first 85

The Hell Gate explosion on October 10, 1885, when nine acres of rock obstructions to navigation were blasted out of Hell Gate Channel. *The Hell Gate Explosion, 1885. Museum of the City of New York.*

started coasting. Some of the rocks and shoals are named after ships that had been lost on them—Great Eastern Rock off eastern Long Island in the shadow of Montauk Point; Cerberus Shoal midway between Long Island and Fisher's Island; Nebraska Shoal off the south shore of Rhode Island; and many others. Woods Hole, the Race and Hell Gate, narrow bottlenecks with swift tides and dangerous rips, were treated with great respect. Traffic streaming in and out of New York through Hell Gate with its strong, sometimes six-knot current, made navigation extremely difficult. Coasting schooners often had to anchor and wait for the tide or accept a tow. But that evening the tide was right, according to Jack Jenkinson, and at dusk the *Norris* drifted through the passage under short canvas and pulled up alongside a wharf at South Street to lay in for the night.

It was just getting dark when a burly longshoreman came running down the wharf waving his lantern. "Get that hand puller the hell outta here," he shouted at Zeb, who looked up mildly while continuing to put the stops on the mainsail.

"Get that Goddam junk offa here or I'll cut your lines," he snarled, moving closer and pulling a knife from his pocket.

Zeb hopped ashore and ambled slowly towards the man, who held up the flickering lantern as he approached. The skipper of the *Norris* towered over the longshoreman. Raising his huge hands up to the man's face, Zeb spoke in a slow, calm voice, "Mister, I just wisht you weighed a ton." The longshoreman considered this remark in stunned silence, then spun on his heel, fled down the pier and disappeared into the night.

New York's South Street in those days was a forest of masts and a jungle of spars and rigging. The jib booms of square-riggers arched up over the street. A big fishing fleet crowded Fulton Market Wharf. Cape Horn grain ships; proud, jaunty tugs with carved eagles adorning their cabins; barges, canal boats and steamships; vessels of every registry crowded against the wharves. Barrels, bails, boxes, lumber and chain were heaped up everywhere. Pungent East Indian spices, tea from China, coffee from South America, fish, tar, hemp and even the ever-present dray horses richly perfumed the air. Stevedores shouted, block and tackle creaked and sails snapped. Hawkers

Cargo schooners being loaded and unloaded at South Street piers in about 1895. *Photo: Alice Austen Collection, Staten Island Historical Society.*

peddled everything from sea chests to suspenders, often pilfered from cargoes being loaded or unloaded. Ship chandlers, sail lofts, grog shops, saloons and boarding houses lined the cobblestone streets.

Dance halls flourished along with tattoo parlors, skittel alleys, tailor shops and brothels such as the "Shimmy and Drawers" and "The Black and Tan Concert Hall" (the latter allowing men of color). It was raw and rough—life was cheap. Even a small coaster wasn't free from waterfront predators. While the captain was being paid for his cargo, thieves would sometimes insert a hose into the cabin of the schooner. When the captain and crew turned in for the night, the thief would pipe in a gas, rendering all hands on board unconscious and easy marks for robbery.

There was much to see, to smell, to hear, and watch out for as Zeb cruised the waterfront. The coasterman's reaction to New York was apt to differ from that of the deepwater sailor. He was, first of all, his own man. Because he was in port frequently, unlike the deepwater sailor, his hunger for women wasn't as fierce. The more reckless and footloose deepwater men were sitting ducks for thieving prostitutes, crimps and crooked saloonkeepers, who could knock them off in a matter of minutes.

Zeb was hardly immune to temptation, though, and one can only guess to what degree he indulged himself in New York. In any event, both he and Jack survived the night, got the barrels unloaded in the morning, and sailed around the tip of Manhattan to Perth Amboy to take aboard a load of coal for New Bedford.

He frequently repeated this run. The following winter, on such a trip, the *Norris* became frozen in the ice at City Island. Zeb, being a restless person by nature, decided after a few days to hire someone to keep an eye on the stranded vessel so he could return to the Vineyard. As soon as the ice had begun to break, Zeb asked his nephew Tom Tilton to accompany him back to New York to pick up the *Norris*. They traveled on the Fall River Line's paddle steamer *The Commonwealth* from New Bedford. Nicknamed "Queen of the Sound," she was a magnificent sight, a veritable floating palace. Elegantly dressed passengers mingled in the main salon while the strains of a stringed orchestra accompanied the gentle splash of her giant paddles.

**SCENES OF
THE PORT OF NEW YORK
ABOUT 1900**

ABOVE: A patron and an employee of the Black and Tan Concert Hall on Broome Street, circa 1890. *Photo: Jacob A. Riis Collection (#163), Museum of the City of New York.* RIGHT: New York police hunting dock rats. *Photo: Jacob A. Riis Collection, Museum of the City of New York.* OPPOSITE, BELOW: New York Harbor. *Courtesy of the South Street Seaport Museum.* OPPOSITE, ABOVE: (left to right) A harbor scavenger and a longshoreman. A woman collecting pieces of tree bark. *Photos: George Bradford Brainerd, Brooklyn Museum—Brooklyn Public Library—Brooklyn Collection.* A shack housing a donkey engine used to load and unload cargo on a New York pier. *Photo: Robert Lee, courtesy of the South Street Seaport Museum.* A street peddler on the waterfront. *Alice Austen Collection, Staten Island Historical Society.*

A number of decorative styles went into her creation—the grand salon was done in Gothic, the garden cafe on the main deck had a Parisian motif and the dining room— her masterpiece—on the upper deck fifty feet above the water, was enclosed with glass under a great domed ceiling. There were oriental carpets and plush velvet throughout.

In spite of, or perhaps because of, all *The Commonwealth's* luxuries, Zeb and Tom headed for the fo'c's'le, where Zeb assured him they'd find a more congenial bed. Tom, however, needed only one look at the tough clientele crammed in the fo'c's'le to know that it might be a perilous night. "Hold on," he warned Zeb, "we're hiring a stateroom. I ain't sleepin' there." Better quarters were acquired to ease Tom's mind and the schooner was retrieved without incident.

In addition to Tom Tilton's occasional help, Zeb continued to have the services of several others; Manuel Sylvia and Jack Jenkinson in particular. Although both men worked hard, neither one could be expected to be the equal of Zeb in strength or in seamanship. Most of the time Zeb was a patient and agreeable skipper. There were limits, however, to his tolerance. One afternoon on Long Island Sound, Zeb decided to try once again to teach Manuel the points of the compass. As before, Manuel shook his head, confused. Finally, in desperation, Zeb asked, "For God's sakes, Manuel, what would you do if I died right here and now?"

For a moment Manuel retreated into this dark and gloomy thought. "I'd die too, Zeb," he finally mumbled, displaying the depth of his loyalty to the captain's example.

On that particular trip, Zeb was unusually anxious to get back to New Bedford. Of all the skippers on the coast, he had been singled out by the Fox Film Company in 1916 to perform a particularly difficult feat for the movie, *Down to the Sea in Ships*, starring Clara Bow. Someone was needed with enough skill to race a two-masted schooner under full sail right up alongside a wharf, nearly nick the corner dolphin and run on down the river. In return for Zeb's feat, the Fox Film Company was to pay to have the vessel overhauled. It was an advantageous arrangement and as soon as Zeb arrived in New Bedford, he had the old vessel up on the ways getting a new coat of paint. When she had slipped back into the water with masts and rigging repaired or renewed as well, a load of whale oil casks was lashed on her foredeck. Zeb viewed this theatrical addition with amusement. It certainly didn't add to the *Norris'* looks as far as he was concerned.

LEFT: An interior view of the elegant steamer *Commonwealth. Courtesy of the Fall River Historical Society.* BELOW: Clara Bow and an unidentified actor in a scene from *Down to the Sea in Ships. Courtesy of the New Bedford Whaling Museum.*

On the appointed day, with cameras set up on the wharf, an actor came aboard and stood on the foredeck. He was to leap from the rail as the schooner passed the wharf and, following the script, chase a man down the pier.

There was a grey, lowering sky with blustery winds as the *Norris* dutifully bore down on the pier. The actor took one look at the leap he was supposed to make, blanched and lost his nerve. Zeb swung on by, ran down the river and repeated the scene, again passing the corner dolphin with only inches to spare. Again the actor hesitated and failed to jump. Zeb was beginning to lose his patience; he had little use for people who postponed things. Again he turned on down the river and back for another try. With her sails arched and white foam churning under her bow, Zeb stood lightly at the schooner's wheel in his shirt sleeves. The *Norris* had just about all the wind she could handle; her deck was canted, and the sheets and shrouds sang under the strain of the whistling northwester. The actor stood on the rail, pale and drawn, while Zeb calmly chattered to himself as he timed the approach. This time the *Norris'* bow actually struck the corner piling a glancing blow. The actor popped into the air like a grasshopper, missed the dock and fell in the water. While he was being fished out, Zeb and the *Norris* vanished down-river, bound for home in disgust.

Zeb had no regrets over discarding this chance for new glamour and glory. He had already made his reputation the hard way and valued it more than any other claim to fame. Yet in December, 1917, the men on the New Bedford waterfront heard him say he'd fill a contract to freight brick from Greenport, Long Island, to New Bedford and be home in time for Christmas. With only ten days to accomplish this feat, they considered it was one boast that Zeb couldn't meet. Three runs were necessary with eight hours required to load each time and a day and a half to unload. The likelihood of sleet, ice or gale winds was very real and the possibility of success seemed most unlikely.

When they sailed, Zeb's daughter Rosalie, now fourteen and a chip off the old block, was along. She was sturdy at the helm or at manning the pumps, alert on the halyards, nimble at reefing and a good cook besides. It was well known that Zeb could handle ten brick at a time, to the average man's five or six, and that he could work day and night with almost no sleep. Even so, there were doubters aplenty as the job began. Zeb and his mate made every second count. As the last of the brick came aboard for each load, the mainsail was rising on the mast, while Rosalie tended the wheel. Winds

OPPOSITE: Rosalie Tilton and her brother Everett in 1912. *Courtesy of Rosalie Tilton Spence.* RIGHT: The *John B. Norris* in her prime. *Peabody Essex Museum.*

favored the whole time, blowing a gale night and day during all three trips between Greenport and New Bedford. To the disbelief of all, they pulled into Vineyard Haven Harbor on Christmas Eve. "We made furrow and harrow marks in the water what didn't smooth over for three weeks," Zeb chuckled to his brother.

Though Zeb and the *Norris* had triumphed, the unusually severe winter took its toll elsewhere. There was little open water that year between Martha's Vineyard and Nantucket. Time and again schooners bringing in supplies had to turn back when the ice began to close in around them. Time and again the steamboats were stalled waiting for a change in tide or weather to ease the frozen sea. A passing steamer crew noticed that the ice pack had closed in around the Cross Rip Lightship. The steamboat could approach near enough to throw newspapers to the vessel, but no closer. For four days the steamboat captains and the keeper of the Greater Point Light sought some means of rescue for the six men aboard. On the fifth day, the keeper realized that the lightship was slowly being carried out to sea. With her flag flying the signal of distress, the ill-fated men must have watched in horror while the island passed from view. The ice field moved inch by inch, foot by foot, towards the dreaded shoals to the east. Only when the weather broke could a search be made for her, but the lightship was never found. It was assumed she touched bottom on Bass Rip, or Rose and Crown Shoal and had been forced under by the ice. The hazards of storm and sea were not to be lightly dismissed, yet for men like Zeb Tilton such dangers were the accepted conditions of their profession. Year after year, in all seasons and in almost any weather, the wind-driven schooners doggedly continued to carry the freight.

Zeb remained a familiar character in every port up and down the coast. Vessels like the *John B. Norris* and the *Wilfred J. Fuller* before her were not, however, as durable as their skippers. By 1921, Zeb's schooner was nearly worn out. As luck would have it, soon after the *Norris* was sold down east, the one schooner which was the real love of Zeb's life came up for sale. Arthur Stevens, her owner, needed something bigger—a three-master capable of carrying more tonnage. Zeb had kept in touch with Stevens since his earlier employment, which doubtless gave him an edge as a likely purchaser. And besides, some prosperous years with the *Norris* enabled Zeb to afford the $4500 price. Now, after fifteen years since their first encounter, the *Alice S. Wentworth* would be his at last.

ABOVE: Looking forward on the *Alice*, running before the wind "wung out." *Photo: Charles F. Sayle.*
LEFT: John Leavitt's rendering of the cabin in the *Alice S. Wentworth. Courtesy of Mystic Seaport and Wesleyan University Press.*

VI

FAIR *ALICE*

They were both in their prime that summer of 1921—the *Alice* was fifty-eight and Zeb fifty-four. Unlike most schooners which had carried heavy cargoes for years, her sheer line still described a graceful, inverted arc, as slim as in her youth. And Zeb's talent for handling white duck and yellow pine was a matter of record. Some said that now Zeb had her, they'd go anywhere it was damp.

Zeb made arrangements with Captain Stevens to pick up the schooner in New Bedford. Although Stevens had a Fairbanks Morse Bulldog engine on the deck for hoisting sail and a yawl boat with a "one lunger" in her for pushing the vessel, these were deleted from the sale.

The *Alice* was worth waiting for. Above the four bunks in the spacious cabin was the same fine paneling, matching the floor, which Zeb had so admired before. Ample space existed between the black iron cookstove and the kitchen table and chairs, which were fixed against the after bulkhead. Counters and dish lockers were set against the forward bulkhead. Seat lockers extended in front of the berths on each side and partly across the after bulkhead on the port side to provide a landing for the companionway ladder. Gimballed lamps were set on the forward and after bulkheads. Plenty of daylight came through the large overhead skylight and the ports in the sides of the cabin.

The *Wentworth* had retained her huge rig after she'd been rebuilt by Captain Stevens. Such an enormous sail area was typical of Long Island Sound schooners which normally are subject to relatively light winds. With such a rig, her shoal draft and her huge oak centerboard, she was still as fine a sailor as ever before. Without motorized accessories, she was now a "hand puller" again, and Zeb was delighted. "It takes brains to run a schooner, but anybody can run an engine," he reminded Jack Jenkinson. Nonetheless engines were surely coming into their own.

The New England Steamship Company's first steamboat that could comfortably carry automobiles was running to the island that August. Trucks were moving more of the freight up and down the eastern seaboard as blacktop roads spread their tentacles along the coast. The railroads, not directly linking the cities, diverted more and more cargo away from coastwise schooners. Tugs with two or three barges trailing a mile astern were plowing coastal waterways, their carrying capacity far beyond that of any schooner. Many of the barges were actually old sailing vessels which had been cut down, with only small leg-o'-mutton sails to steady them in heavy weather. As tall clip-

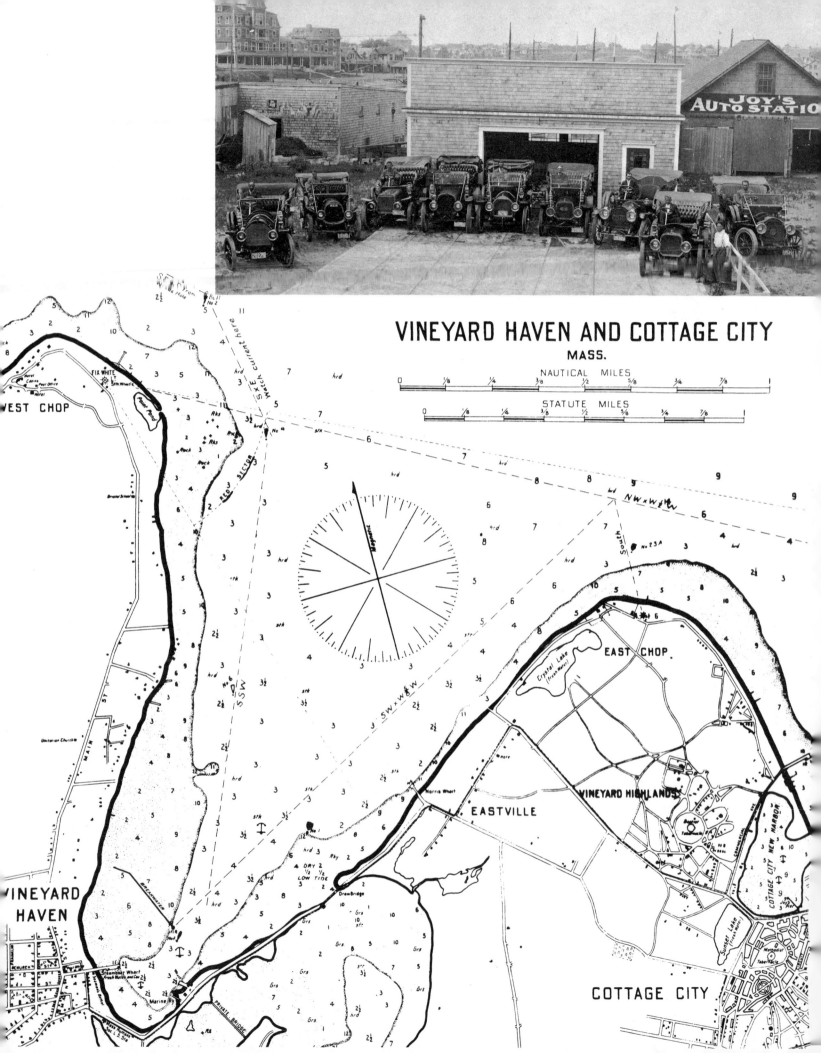

VINEYARD HAVEN AND COTTAGE CITY
MASS.

NAUTICAL MILES

STATUTE MILES

OPPOSITE, BELOW: A detail from the 1920 *Eldridge Tide and Pilot Book*. OPPOSITE, ABOVE: Cars for hire in Cottage City. *Courtesy of the Vineyard Gazette.* RIGHT: A corner of Edgartown Harbor in the 1920s illustrating the fact that some elements may never change. *Photo: Clara F. Dinsmore, courtesy of the Vineyard Gazette.*

per ships with snowy canvas piled tier upon tier, they had been proud and beautiful creations. Stripped of their life-giving sail, only a mournful memory of former glory remained.

Vineyarders in general, however, were not easily convinced that new technology and sophisticated ways were necessary or desirable. While the tourists may have exposed the island to the latest mainland style in dress, music and attitudes, such influences took root offshore only with extreme difficulty. A young Vineyard lad, asked to write an essay for school about Julius Caesar, demonstrated the point of view. He concluded his report, "I didn't like him much, and besides, he was an off-islander."

Even the language resisted change. "Housen" were houses, boat was pronounced "bought," a full gale was called a "breeze," a thunderstorm a "tempest" and binoculars were "offshore glasses."

Vineyarders' independence and insistence on their own way remained steadfast. Jessie Tilton, a relative of Zeb's, gave up her acting career with Joseph Jefferson's stage company to run an ice cream parlor in Edgartown. She was noted for the fact that she hated films and complained that "celluloids are cheaper than the clasp on a ten-cent bracelet." In later years, when she became hard of hearing, she entered the town hall to cast her vote in a local election and asked the clerk for help. He drew her aside, asking, "Are you a Democrat or a Republican?" "Yankee!" she boomed in her best stage voice, which carried out to Main Street.

But even such firm Yankee stuff is vulnerable. Some younger Vineyard residents found it exciting to mimic vacationers who, in 1921, swam in revealing black wool bathing suits, bobbed their hair and dabbed on rouge. Youths raced all around the island in the tin lizzies which had replaced the electrics and horse taxis. The *Gazette* reported that the summer had been "especially rich in spills and collisions...." As if all that weren't enough, *Sibley's New Red Trolley Car Steamboat Bus* with penumatic tires and wicker seats now met the ferries at Oak Bluffs.

The Volstead Act passed two years earlier provided a new and somewhat different occupation for those in the fishing fleet endowed with that celebrated Yankee eye for profit. No one was more adept at sailing along the darkened coast than these men, to whom one dollar was as good as another and a fifth of scotch worth many a flounder. Good liquor reached Martha's Vineyard, as it did most of southern New England, regu-

larly via St. Pierre and Miquelon, off the southern coast of Newfoundland, as well as from the West Indies and Bermuda.

"According to the stories of fishermen and yachtsmen," the *Gazette* reported, "rum runners are plying a regular trade between the Vineyard and the mainland. Summer residents on the sound side of the island tell of hearing whistles coming in irregular sequence after dark, as if signalling were on. Old-timers infer the signalling has to do with the moonshine business."

The paper further stated, "Hootch, not home brewed or moonshine, but old fashion 100 proof of every conceivable kind from plain cheap rum to the highest grade is being openly sold and in large quantities within thirty miles of Martha's Vineyard.

"A two-masted schooner, the *Arethusa*, formerly the largest of the Gloucester fishing fleet, but now said to be sailing under British colors, is anchored some ten miles off Noman's Land and for some time past has been the mecca of those Vineyard residents, and others of the thirsty, whose desire for liquid refreshment warrants the long trip to sea. And judging by the amount of business the schooner is doing, their name is legion."

The Women's Christian Temperance Union which opposed such practices was outraged. After all, the ladies argued, didn't Dukes County hold the honor of passing the first liquor law in the country—prohibiting the sale of alcohol to the Indians on the island in 1650!

The swamps of Noman's Land, a small island lying off the tip of Gay Head, were used for storage. Rum runners operated long, low boats equipped with two or three Liberty engines able to make twenty-five knots, which they regularly ran in to Noman's Land from beyond the three-mile limit, and later on twelve-mile limit, at night. From here, the liquor was easily transferred either to the Vineyard or to the mainland. In the 1920's Noman's Land was privately owned and attended only by a hired caretaker who was canny enough not to miss out on this new enterprise; he charged for the use of the swamp.

Although Zeb didn't drink, smoke, or engage in bootlegging, he was vastly amused at the game of tag played between the fishermen and the law. Just as they cast off the lines on one of his first trips with the *Wentworth* out of New Bedford, Zeb dropped a hint that he had a load of "wet goods" aboard.

They sailed unhindered into Vineyard Haven and brought the vessel up along-

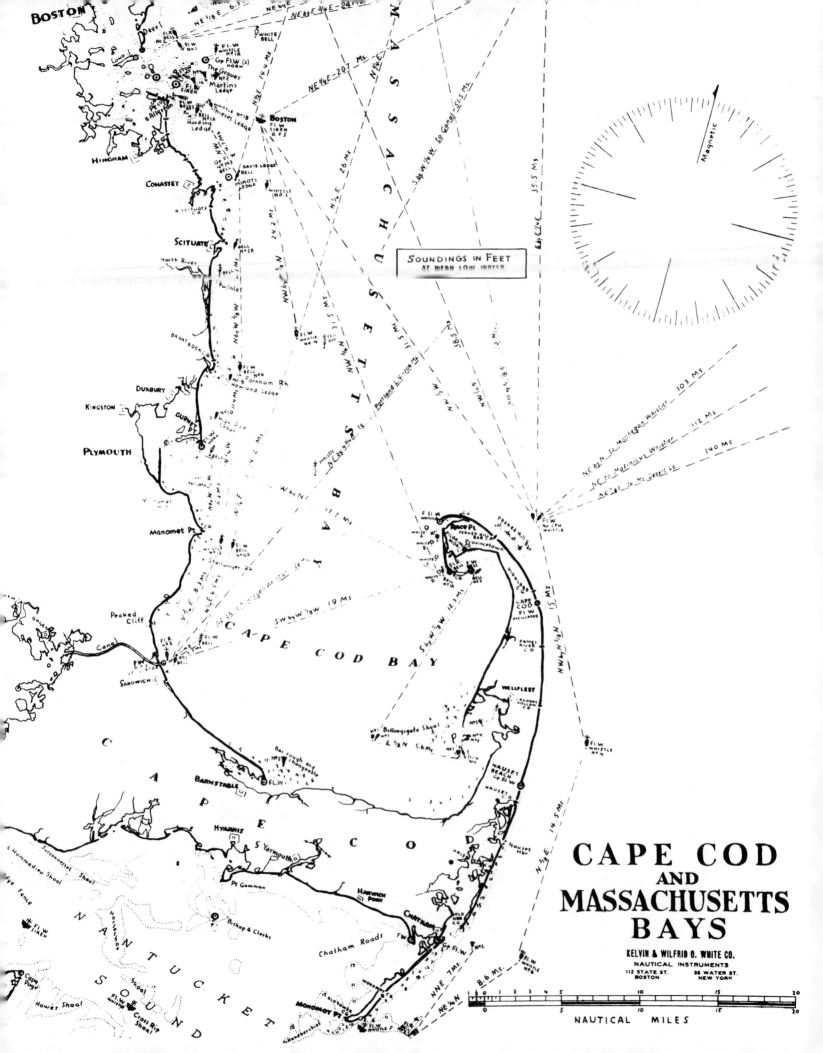

CAPE COD
AND
MASSACHUSETTS BAYS

KELVIN & WILFRID O. WHITE CO.
NAUTICAL INSTRUMENTS
112 STATE ST.   38 WATER ST.
BOSTON   NEW YORK

NAUTICAL MILES

SOUNDINGS IN FEET
AT MEAN LOW WATER

OPPOSITE: A detail from the 1920 *Eldridge Tide and Pilot Book*. RIGHT: The *Alice S. Wentworth* in 1932, with a load of oysters on deck, off Chatham, Mass. *Photo: Walter Love, courtesy of the Vineyard Gazette.*

side the steamboat wharf as usual. Before anyone could furl sail, however, federal agents swarmed aboard. Zeb's elaborately indifferent manner only served to strengthen the deep suspicion surrounding his cargo. Wary New Bedford authorities, who had heard his remark, had phoned the Vineyard to report it. A special trap had been set.

Instantly, two officers demanded that the vessel be searched for "wet goods."

"Well, gentlemen, you be standing on 'em," Zeb drawled as he opened the hatch. The officers peered down at a load of ice. "Them's wet goods, ain't they?" he asked.

It is doubtful that the incident did anything to allay suspicions about Zeb. From then on a careful watch was kept on all his actions, which was, of course, a source of great delight to the captain of the *Alice S. Wentworth*.

By now Zeb was the most famous skipper in southern New England. He was known in all the ports along the coast; the *Wentworth* would be recognized as soon as she came up on the horizon, and by the time they tied up in port, a group would often have gathered around to greet her and marvel at her captain in action. He could leap several feet up onto a wharf, with the same buoyancy as when he had won the long jump races at the Agricultural Fairs in his youth. Because he was so quick and nimble, it is not surprising that he never once fell overboard. Like most men who worked on the water, he never did learn to swim.

Most coasting schooners of the *Wentworth's* size carried two in crew, in addition to the captain, though Zeb felt this was just a waste of money. Routine tacking or jibing offshore was simple. With two in crew, one man remained forward and one aft. When the skipper rolled the wheel hard up and the schooner began to swing off the wind, the mate aft took in the slack on the main sheet and caught a turn on the quarter bit as the huge boom swung over and fetched up with a crash. The hand forward trimmed the headsheets and coiled them down. Zeb, however, handled both the helm and the main himself, while his mate handled the foresail and jibs.

In those days, one of the best cargoes a small schooner could get was oysters to be hauled from Greenport, Long Island, and other unfavorable waters as far south as the Delaware region, up to Chatham on Cape Cod. The young, three-year-old oysters were seeded in Chatham's Stage Harbor and the Oyster River where they grew another year and a half to maturity in clean water and were fit for gourmet consumption as "Chatham oysters" in restaurants of Boston, Providence and New York.

101

LEFT: A three-masted schooner with a load of lumber rounding West Chop under shortened canvas in a stiff breeze. *Photo: Clara F. Dinsmore, courtesy of the Vineyard Gazette.* OPPOSITE: Zeb's house on the North Road in Chilmark in 1930. *Courtesy of Rosalie Tilton Spence.*

When an oyster-laden schooner arrived at Stage Harbor, its cargo was usually unloaded onto scows owned by S.W. Gould & Sons and towed into shallow water for seeding. The season was short, lasting only about six weeks in the spring, so speed multiplied profits for the coastermen. At twenty cents a bushel for freightage, a load of three thousand bushels, such as the *Alice* carried, could turn a nice profit of some nine hundred dollars. It was also an easy cargo to handle, even though the shells had to be kept cool under wetted canvas. Thus competition was keen for the S.W. Gould contracts.

On Zeb's first oyster trip one season, he was ready to sail the minute the last bushel was aboard. When they peaked up the main, the strain was too much for the old canvas of the *Alice,* and it split down the center. Zeb couldn't wait for repairs. Another schooner nearby offered to stay with them for possible assistance as they slipped out of the harbor. Putting on all the remaining canvas she had, the *Alice Wentworth* moved out ahead as they sailed eastward. Zeb kept his narrow lead and when they raised the half-tide rocks at Dry Pigs off Cuttyhunk, he was careful to check the tides. Zeb was going to show who needed assistance. Since they'd be getting a head tide in Vineyard Sound, he ducked inside Buzzards Bay, sailing on up to Woods Hole. When he looked back, the accompanying vessel was barely visible on the horizon, miles down the sound, still bucking the tide.

As soon as all the oysters had been taken off in Chatham and Zeb was paid, the sail, still unrepaired, was up and drawing in no time. Zeb had an amorous appointment in Oak Bluffs which, as usual, he was anxious not to miss. Perhaps he'd grown careless; a bit too casual. In any event, his wife Edith and oldest daughter Rosalie had somehow gotten wind of the affair and they too were headed for the appointed rendezvous, on foot. Along the way, an undertaker friend offered them a ride, whereupon they jumped

into the unoccupied hearse. After their arrival in Oak Bluffs, they parked by the Tivoli Dance Hall. From inside the unlikely conveyance, they spotted Zeb waiting at the steamboat wharf, all done up in smiles as he contemplated an evening with his lady friend, who could be seen walking up the pier to meet him.

The carefree pair meandered along up-street, the woman giggling at Zeb's witty remarks and both unaware that a hearse was following slowly behind. Just as they reached the boarding house where the lady had taken lodgings, the door of the hearse flew open. Out leapt Rosalie and Edith, splitting the air with language that would make a bluefish blush.

Zeb backed off, something he rarely did, and made a hasty retreat to the *Wentworth,* not at all pleased at getting caught at the old sailor's game. "Besides giving me hell, they was plannin' to kill me and take me off for buryin' on the spot," he grumbled to his mate.

Such adventures never interferred with business, which remained brisk for Zeb and the *Alice.* Their specialty was getting through where others wouldn't dare to go. Coming down from New York, Zeb would slip inside the Hen and Chickens Lightship, run through shoal water inside the old Cock Reef and within three hundred feet of the rocks off Horseneck Beach at Westport, saving miles and hours. "It's just a question of knowin' your way around," Zeb once told a friend. "One time we was comin' into Greenport in fog thick as mud—couldn't see ten feet. I tole the boy to throw a line on the spile. 'I don't see no spile,' he calls aft. 'Then jus' reach out,' I tole him. Sure enough, the boy puts his hand right on the timber."

Although Zeb's two sons were now old enough to sail with him when they weren't in school, he still needed a regular mate. His nephew, Tom Tilton, signed on for regular 103

work in 1924, the wisest choice Zeb ever made. Tom had sailed with Zeb a few times on the *Norris* and the *Fuller* when he was a teenager and they complemented each other handsomely. Tom could handle sail almost as easily as Zeb and he liked to keep the vessel in Bristol fashion—something to which Zeb paid only irregular attention.

Although he usually relied on a single mate as crew, Zeb took on a promising young man to serve as all 'round deck hand and cabin boy, to do whatever small chores there were. Walter Love of Chatham signed aboard the *Alice* when he was thirteen, and for two seasons hauled oysters with Zeb, Tom and a cat. Walter claims to have learned more about practical seamanship, navigation and the ways of the coastermen during this time than in all the rest of his years at sea and with the U.S. Coast Guard. Once, while under shortened canvas in a hard gale, Zeb ordered Walter to climb over the stern to untangle a line. He did so and found himself hanging there, unable to climb back again, while the *Alice* pitched in heavy seas. When Zeb finally saw his predicament and pulled him back aboard, Zeb remarked, "If you know nothin', you fears nothin'."

The combination of a reputation for dependability and Zeb's engaging personality gained him and Tom all the contracts they could handle and consequently a very healthy income. They sailed hard and ate well. Water was used sparingly because they never knew when they might be caught offshore, but Zeb even let Tom do the dishes, a privilege accorded few. After a hard day under sail and at work, the comfortable cabin was a delightful refuge. The big grey enamel coffee pot was always filled, ever ready for the almost unbreakable white ironware cups nearby. Like all Tiltons, Zeb had his own theories about the value of certain foods. He never bought, ate, or allowed a tomato on his schooner. Squishy "love apples" without any authority to them, he claimed. If anyone became ill while on his vessel they were fed hot ginger tea. In addition to tea, Zeb was sure that raisins had powerful curative qualities.

During one summer, Tom's ailing daughter Mildred was advised by a doctor to get plenty of rest and sunshine. The pale, sickly child was immediately dispatched to the *Wentworth*. Mildred adored her Uncle Zeb and willingly ate the boxes and boxes of raisins he fed her. The treatment must have worked, for long after that summer, whenever the schooner put into Vineyard Haven, the child would be certain to appear on the dock and clamor aboard.

On one such visit, a cargo of brick had been unloaded. Tom went into town while

Zeb swept the deck with a broom. The water between the vessel and the steamboat wharf was red from the brick dust when Mildred arrived. Just as she tried to jump aboard, the vessel swung away from the wharf; she missed the rail and fell into the harbor. Though she couldn't swim, Mildred somehow managed to grab the barnacle-encrusted piling and yell for help. Zeb stuck his head over the rail to see what was making all the noise.

"Why, if it ain't Millie," he drawled appreciatively. He quickly lowered the business end of the broom down and hauled her aboard dripping wet, covered with scratches and colored red from head to foot.

The child's adoration for Zeb never faltered and it must have been reciprocated for when she graduated from high school Zeb gave her a beautiful pink purse enclosing a twenty-dollar bill and a small box of raisins.

Though Zeb was now fifty-seven years old, his pride was still a harsh taskmaster. When Tom urged him to get a hoisting engine on the *Wentworth*, the skipper refused at first. His mistrust of machinery was still as great as Cleveland's. But performing many jobs by hand was wasting precious time, and besides, Zeb wasn't really aware of how far his own strength exceeded that of the men who worked beside him. Finally Zeb gave in and an old donkey engine was installed just forward of the foremast to raise and lower sails and anchor, and to lift out heavy cargo. The wind, however, would always give him the power he needed to sail. No one ever used a breeze to greater advantage. Secure in this knowledge, Zeb never missed the chance to challenge any other sailing craft to a race.

Zeb and two friends were sailing light down to Greenport one day to pick up a load of oysters, at a time when Tom was not aboard. Once out of the harbor the captain spotted the *Sharpshooter*, a down east vessel in which he knew an engine had been recently installed. This he considered not only a waste of money, but a violation of higher laws as well. After all, the Lord provided wind and it was, of course, free. Quickly, Zeb's crew raised the topsails and the schooner felt the pull as they arched before a strong northeaster. Zeb's friend Lambert Knight, a veteran of the Australian grain races, checked his watch. With all her sails set and her engine billowing black smoke, the *Sharpshooter* took an early lead. Zeb headed up the *Wentworth* and drove her as hard as he dared. As soon as they passed the lee of the island leaving Vineyard Sound, they

OPPOSITE: The *Alice* leaving Vineyard Haven in the early 1930s against a background of the East Chop shore. *Photo: A.B. Merry.* RIGHT: Zeb posing at the wheel of the *Alice* while the schooner was tied up in Nantucket in the 1930s. *Courtesy of Charles F. Sayle.*

caught the full force of the gale. Zeb muttered incessantly to the *Alice*, urging her on, steadying her kicking wheel as he kept her as close to the wind as possible. She began to gain, boiling along at better than ten knots. Soon they were only about a boat length behind the *Sharpshooter* and continuing to close the gap. As they passed Fisher's Island, the strain on her canvas was such that the foretopsail blew out. Zeb made no move to take in the other topsail and on they went, not only passing the other craft but leaving her puffing far astern. Zeb swung up into Greenport Harbor, dropped anchor and sails, and waited for the *Sharpshooter*. Lambert Knight raced ashore to call the Vineyard and verify the time. They had made the run, 110 air miles, in seven and a half hours. It was a record never equalled by any other coasting schooner.

The wind, which served Zeb so faithfully, was nonetheless a fickle partner. A friend of Zeb's, finding himself becalmed, tossed a quarter in the sea to encourage a breeze. Within the hour, a fierce storm arose which cost the sailor both his masts.

"If I'd known wind was so cheap," he said later, "I'd have thrown in but a penny."

Repairs were unavoidable. Zeb had his schooner hauled once a year to at least repaint the hull, and usually had this work done in Greenport. Not only did she get a fresh coat of paint but on one occasion Zeb had ordered a new anchor as well. As soon as the *Wentworth* slipped back down the ways, they were ready to move back out into the harbor to load. Zeb was anxious to get going and impatient because the chandler hadn't delivered the new anchor. At last he stomped up the wharf, and a short time later, as Tom reports it, Zeb was seen coming back, walking very slowly, with the anchor over his shoulder. It weighed six hundred pounds.

When her bottom was fresh and her new anchor was drawn up to the cathead on her port bow, Zeb decided he'd repaint the decks. The planks were scarred and blistered and an inch of old paint needed to be removed by the painstakingly slow method of chipping and scraping. When they got to the hatch covers, Zeb felt he had to speed things up. Gasoline was poured on them and set afire. In an instant, Zeb doused the flames with buckets of water before the wood was burned. The old paint was thus consumed, and as soon as the hatches were dry, Zeb happily slapped on the paint.

Tom now went after Zeb to get an auxiliary yawl boat with an engine. Again it was hard to convince him. Zeb insisted that wind and tide were all he needed and that machinery couldn't be trusted.

107

ABOARD THE *ALICE S. WENTWORTH* IN THE 1930s.

Photos: Courtesy of Charles F. Sayle.

OPPOSITE: Gale Huntington, who played the guitar as well as the fiddle, entertaining his daughter Emily, in a painting done by Thomas Hart Benton in 1940. *Lithograph, courtesy of Emily Huntington Rose.* RIGHT: The *Wentworth* tied up at the wharf in Vineyard Haven. *Photo: Clara F. Dinsmore, courtesy of the Vineyard Gazette.*

"There ain't half the number of persons what perished in the coasting trade as dies from automobilin'. Boys these days would rather run around in an automobile instead of doing a day's work aboard a schooner. They want to be home nights to meet their girls as if there wa'n't one in every port. I oughta know. Why, Henry Ford is killin' the country."

Yet Tom was right. Zeb again eventually agreed that he would have to have a yawl boat with power if he was going to continue to compete. Reflecting his regret at this necessity, Zeb reminisced about the old days with the yard man who was installing the two-cylinder Lathrop engine on the yawl boat. "When you went over the Nantucket shoals with fifty sail alongside," he recalled, "it was like a regatta and some sport too. When you put in to Vineyard Haven Harbor with a hundred other schooners and every one was so close you was almost deck and deck alongside, you knew you were in a world of consequences."

The shipyard bill was always far beyond the most careful estimate. Zeb's eyes pulled in towards his nose and his huge hand curled around his chin as he examined it slowly and carefully. "I think that pencil you got must be split," he muttered to the bookkeeper, "'cause every time you write down one, it comes out two." Cost, however, was unimportant when it came to caring for the *Alice*. To Zeb, money was to be used and not just counted. Like getting the full benefit of the tide, he wanted to make the most of every living moment.

With her new yawl boat, the *Wentworth* maintained an edge on all schooners her size and Zeb did manage to put away a little money. In spite of the fact that many tried, with considerable success, to get it away from him, he had saved enough to build a house in Vineyard Haven. On May 15, 1930, the town was astir with the news that Zeb was having an old-fashioned house warming. Over one hundred persons attended, coming from Nantucket, New Bedford and all over the Vineyard. Music was supplied by Wally Long of Nantucket and Artie Look from Chilmark on accordion, two guitarists and Ed Leonard at the piano. Gale Huntington brought his fiddle. Zeb's brother, William, opened the evening with some deepwater chanteys and then stepped out on the floor to do a jig. When a group began a square dance, the windows rattled and the sills shook as the boys beat out "Buffalo Girls," "Roll Down to Rio," "Soldiers' Joy" and "Money Musk," Zeb had freighted in a load of oysters himself, and all hands were

111

served while the dancing and laughter rang through the night. They feasted until the moon had set and the east was getting light, at which time Zeb was up as usual and gone on the early tide.

Later that season a contract to carry paving oil from New Jersey to New Bedford was acquired and still another nephew, Alton Tilton, came along. They pulled into New Bedford and tied up at the Fairhaven Bridge to unload, as usual. By the time the drums were off the *Wentworth's* deck, Zeb's clothes—the only ones he had—were coated with oil. He gave Alton some money and told him to go uptown and buy a new set of long underwear, pants and a shirt. Zeb then went below, stripped, and tossed all his oily attire up through the companionway and into the harbor. Naked as a newborn babe, he sat in the cabin waiting for Alton. Restlessness set in rapidly; Zeb had some visiting to do. Periodically he'd peer up the companionway to see autos rumbling over the bridge. The passengers would peer back and force Zeb to retreat from view. He was trapped and getting more impatient by the minute. Finally a friend came along. "For God's sakes go uptown and find Alton," yelled Zeb. The friend had never seen the old skipper in such a compromising position and intended to make the most of it. Alton, who had been instructed to take his time, returned at a leisurely pace. Late or not, Zeb leapt into his new attire and sped angrily off. Even at the age of sixty-three, nothing could stand in the way of romance ashore.

Zeb, however, never left his vessel for very long. He felt there was a degenerating influence to land. If he had a few days between contracts in the summer, Zeb would ask a gang of friends to accompany him on a pleasure cruise over towards Nantucket, or westward to Gay Head and Noman's Land. "This here's my hobby and my living," he explained whenever someone asked him why he didn't spend more time ashore.

To outsiders it seemed that Zeb often took unnecessary chances, but he was more at home afloat than ashore and was fully aware of the nature of each gamble. In this respect *Alice* served him well, although they did have a few close calls together. The year before, they were coming up Vineyard Sound on the night of August 27 with a deck-load of road oil when they ran into a heavy squall. It was a storm just like many storms Zeb had seen before, so he simply shortened sail and kept on through torrents of rain with lightning burning the sky. Zeb stood at the wheel, sharp salt spray arching over the deck load and into his face. Suddenly lightning cracked, forking the sky just

overhead and illuminating the deck bright as day. The topmast snapped as a blazing bolt streaked down a backstay and a glare of blue flame ran around the rim of the iron wheel Zeb was holding, blistering the paint and sheering a spoke clean off in his hands. For a second he was stunned and knocked back, but instantly he took the wheel again.

When he sailed into Vineyard Haven Harbor the next morning with the topmast dangling, Zeb explained that it had to have been his rubber boots that saved his life, or that, "I musta had more electricity in me than 'twas in that bolt, else I don't know how it coulda spared me."

Another brush with disaster had occurred one bitter February day in 1928 when the *Wentworth* was bound in from New York with a load of plumbing supplies and asbestos shingles piled on the deck. Zeb, Tom and Alton were all aboard. Sailing down Long Island Sound, a southwest breeze came on. The wind freshened to a gale, bringing snow and sleet.

Once he had a cargo moving, it took a lot of dirty weather to stop Zeb, but he knew they couldn't make Vineyard Haven in the darkening storm, which rapidly closed in around them. He put inside the breakwater at the western end of Point Judith. As they came up into the wind, Tom let go the light anchor on the starboard bow, heaving over as much chain as possible. A piece of jib was hoisted to swing the bow to port and the big anchor was let go. By the time they'd taken a couple of turns around the bits with the icy chain and put stops on the sails, the wind was shrieking through the rigging at eighty to ninety knots. The seas cobbled up sending sheets of grey-green water surging over her deck load. Zeb knew the holding ground was poor, but could do nothing but stand on deck waiting to feel if she'd hold. The sea strained at her anchors until

114

Sunday Journal

Artgrauure Section

TWO PARTS—12 PAGES

SCHOONER ASHORE! In a gale estimated to have had over a 100-mile-an-hour velocity, the Schooner Alice S. Wentworth went ashore off Point Judith during the storm last week. This photograph shows the breeches buoy in position to rescue the crew of the helpless ship. (Upper right) Crews of the Narragansett Pier and the Point Judith stations with Captain C. H. Collins at the gun used to fire the breeches buoy rope.
Journal photos, Goward

LEFT: The *Wentworth's* near disaster off Point Judith was front page news in 1928 in the *Providence Sunday Journal. Courtesy of Mrs. F.S. Gould, collection of the author.* FAR LEFT: Charles Sayle up the foremast of the *Wentworth. Courtesy of Rosalie Tilton Spence.*

Zeb's fears were confirmed and the light one let go. The big anchor wasn't enough to hold and the schooner began to drag until she was fetching up on a rock ledge with every roll.

Zeb knew no one could get off the vessel alive, but if they stayed aboard it was only a question of time before the *Alice* would break up on the rocks. The combers were mounting in the shoal water, exploding against the breakwater and hurling spray thirty feet in the air. Zeb had only one choice. Tom stayed at the wheel while Alton and Zeb crept forward on hands and knees to avoid being swept overboard. A man, if he could swim, would only survive about four minutes in that water. Zeb slipped the chain on the anchor while Alton let the downhaul go and the wind angrily snapped up the jib. Fortunately the wind was on her quarter. If not, they would have had to try and raise the mainsail as the *Wentworth* headed down towards the beach. The seas were hitting them broadside, breaking over the weather rail and filling the dory on deck. When he saw his chance, Zeb rolled the wheel hard over and the three men dashed for the cabin. The schooner hit the beach head on, rose and fell in the following seas breaking over her stern, and seemed to crawl ashore, skidding along on the slippery rocks. Finally the *Wentworth* struck bottom hard, snapping off the rudder.

They had come in on a full tide, and soon the seas began to fall off fast; Zeb was quickly certain that they were safe. Later a Coast Guard vessel arrived at the scene and shot them a breeches buoy which got tangled in the rigging. Zeb was disgusted, and had no intention of having some clumsy character from the federal government remove him from his schooner in that fashion. He insisted they come ashore in the dory.

After staying three days at the Coast Guard Station while a fishing boat assisted in removing the cargo, the *Alice S. Wentworth* was at last pulled off the beach. With a 115

heavy chain dropped off her stern acting as a rudder, she was towed into New London for repairs. The lightkeeper at Point Judith later told Zeb that he had helplessly watched the whole drama, certain all would be lost.

Though several men sailed with Zeb and shared his adventures off and on, the job of regular mate continued to be handled by Tom until 1932, when he left the vessel to go into commercial fishing. After that, Zeb's sons-in-law, John Olsen and Ed Leonard, as well as his daughters, Rosalie, Gertrude, and Ruth sailed with him now and then. The Depression had gripped the nation; unemployment reached thirteen million. There were sit-down strikes, hundreds sold apples in the streets, and Amelia Earhart disappeared. The Lindbergh kidnapping touched the lives of everyone, even the crew of the *Alice*. The intermediary in the case had announced that the baby was on a boat in Vineyard waters and, on several occasions when one of Zeb's daughters was aboard with a baby, the child's cries brought federal authorities aboard the schooner as the desperate manhunt for the kidnapper continued.

The Depression did not spare the Vineyard. Christian Marthinusen, a lean, raw-boned Norwegian who had gone to sea on square-rigged ships when he was thirteen, had later come to this country and settled on the Vineyard. To this day, Charlie, as Marthinusen was called, remembers sitting in the kitchen of his little salt box house in Chilmark one evening, sadly disturbed about the fact that he was jobless, still weak from a two-month's illness in the Marine Hospital in Boston, and had a wife and two children to support. There seemed little chance of finding work.

The kitchen door burst open and Zeb's huge frame filled the entrance.

"Want to make a hundred dollars?" Zeb asked in a gruff voice.

"You might as well say a million," the Norwegian replied. "I'm still pretty weak."

"Well, we leave with the tide in the morning," Zeb drawled and left as quickly as he had come. Charlie accepted what he knew was a generous offer and quickly regained both his strength and his spirits as the new mate of the *Alice S. Wentworth*.

Running light to New York to fetch a load of soft coal, Zeb and his new mate spent the night in New London. In the morning they were greeted with a stiff southeaster. Charlie noticed that the other schooner captains waited to see what Zeb was going to do before deciding to break out their anchors. When they saw him leave, some followed suit. They sailed on down into the sound and met a head tide with a 117

heavy swell coming in by the Race. The old vessel took water over the knighthead on every roll as the wind freshened. Charlie had the wheel and Zeb, who had been making himself some tea, appeared in the gangway.

"Jibe her," he said, and again disappeared below. Charlie thought his skipper had gone mad. To do that would rip the sails to shreds or snap the boom. He held his course. Zeb leapt back up the companionway with a yell. "I said jibe her."

"You'll take the rig right out." Charlie protested.

"Dammit, I said to jibe," Zeb growled, and took Charlie by the front of the shirt with one hand, lifted him off his feet and put him aside. With his left hand on the wheel and his right holding the four lengths of heavy main sheet, Zeb jibed the vessel over. As he did, the sheet sang through the palm of his hand. Charlie was sure he'd ripped off all the skin, but he underestimated his skipper. "That's the way it's done on this vessel," Zeb said calmly, and they returned to New London to wait out the weather.

Like Tom before him, Charlie proved to be an excellent mate, and this was the first and only time the two disagreed. Both Zeb and his wife provided well for Charlie and his family. "I don't know how he found out sometimes, but he always did," Charlie says, "and whatever my wife needed was always there."

OPPOSITE: Charlie Sayle. *Photo: A.B. Merry.*
ABOVE: Music and dancing on the *Wentworth.*
Courtesy of Rosalie Tilton Spence. RIGHT: Charlie
Marthinusen and his concertina. *Photo: A.B.
Merry.*

Though Zeb's regular business suffered during the Depression, he found other ways to pick up a day's pay. He'd berth the *Alice* at the Old South Wharf in Nantucket, clean her up, wash her down and hang a sign in the rigging offering sailing parties every day from 10 A.M. to 5 P.M. at two dollars per person. Thirty or forty people would sign up. Charlie Marthinusen, or Zeb's blind friend Wally Long playing his concertina, would provide the music. Charlie Sayle, another of Zeb's Nantucket friends, also joined the crew for these excursions.

Zeb's personal parties in Nantucket were the best social events of all. His friends could spot the old schooner before she'd rounded Brandt Point, coming in with a load of firewood, quahaug shells, lumber or coal. By the time Zeb had her unloaded, a group would have gathered 'round, and a party would be in the making.

Zeb usually put a big pot of chowder on the back of the stove, baked up some biscuits and gingerbread, and boiled gallons of coffee. Waitresses from the local hotels would always join the fun. If it was good weather, they'd sweep and wash down the foredeck, Wally, Charlie and Herbie Brownell would begin to play, and the dancing would commence. Someone would step out to do the Scottish sword dance, followed by German or Irish jigs and reels, or even the two-step. Around the deck they'd whirl for half the night.

119

The Cobbler's Dance was all Zeb professed to know. With his friends urging him on, his great legs would kick out in time with the tune, as ably as any Cossack's. The Portland Fancy was another favorite. Around the mainmast they'd go, though Zeb's dancing in this case was an awkward walk to which his partner would vainly try to add a little rhythm.

There were other diversions besides dancing for which Zeb was better equipped. On one trip they came into Nantucket with a load of coal. Zeb was a filthy black and went below to change his clothes for the party. The deck was crowded as usual, so he closed the companionway. Soon there was a tap.

"Who might that be?" Zeb asked.

"I'm at your service, Captain Zeb," explained a coy female voice.

Zeb was momentarily surprised. The voice was strange, but he liked the sound of it.

"What kind of service do you give?" Zeb asked blandly.

"Any service you would like Cap," the voice replied.

"Well, come on down," replied Zeb, who was sixty-four years old at the time. "You might be disappointed, but again, you might be damn surprised." The companionway opened, the visitor slipped below, and Zeb closed it behind her. The party on deck progressed without him for a spell.

Zeb loved to freight for the Nantucketers and was pleased, in January of 1934, to get a job bringing in materials for a new Coast Guard Station on the island. The contractor phoned Zeb. "I'll arrive in Oak Bluffs in the morning to talk over the details with you. I wonder if we can't have someone there at the ticket office to identify you?"

"Don't you worry one bit about that, Mister," answered Zeb. "If you have a contract to build a life-saving station on Nantucket in the winter time, I can pick you out in any crowd!" Zeb got to the ferry and recognized the victim immediately.

Norman Benson, an old Vineyard friend, happened to be in Nantucket one time that winter and Zeb offered to give him a rid back home. Norman excelled at trap fishing as Zeb did at coasting. Norman was particularly noted for the live eels he kept in his cellar to be sold to fisherman for bait. To get the eels, he chopped up horseshoe crabs with an axe to bait his traps. Norman also did a little painting and had, years before, put the last coat on the hull of Joshua Slocum's *Spray* before Slocum made his final solo voyage in 1909 from which he never returned.

121

The ice was thick around the harbor when Zeb and Norman left Nantucket and huge floes clogged the sound. They were half way to the Vineyard when they spotted a particularly huge floe dead ahead. "I think we can break her," Zeb told Norman, and the old schooner plowed forward, splitting the ice and up-ending the smaller chunks. But the ice was thicker than Zeb had anticipated, and when the wind fell off, the old vessel was soon frozen fast. They spent the night caught in the ice quite unconcerned. Zeb knew the steamer would be by in the morning on its way to Nantucket. Indeed, she arrived on schedule and altered course, coming in close enough to break up the ice, and they were soon under way again.

Cooperation between working schooners and the steamers was not at all unusual. Men who earn their living on the sea have many basic interests in common. Their fraternity has always pointedly excluded yachtsmen, who have often, in turn, been somewhat condescending toward merchantmen. Joseph Conrad, speaking of this division, wrote of "the fellowship of the craft, which no amount of enthusiasm for yachting, cruising and so on can give, since one is only the amusement of life and the other is life itself."

The merchant sailors' scorn, however, did not prevent them from frequently racing pleasure craft. If the conditions were right, Zeb and the *Alice* would often challenge a yacht and win. When John Leavitt was on the *Wentworth* in Maine, they raced a schooner yacht up the coast all night, beating her handily into port.

In the summer of 1934, the *Wentworth* probably startled yachtsmen more than any other time in her career, when she came boiling into Narragansett Bay during the America's Cup Race trials. Flying light with the wind on her quarter, something that agreed with the old schooner, the *Alice* sailed right through the spectator fleet coming in from the races. Zeb headed straight for the stone bulkhead at Fort Adams which was crowded with spectators. He brought the schooner in so close that when he swung the wheel over, the bowsprit swept in at the throng, scattering them like a flock of chickens. Proceeding unconcerned, he came to anchor in the middle of Newport Harbor, which was packed with vessels of every description.

While Zeb sat on the deck of the *Wentworth* close by the cup defender *Rainbow*, President Franklin Delano Roosevelt relaxed aboard the Astor yacht, *Nourmahal*. On every side were elegant craft crowded with prominent people. An indication of Zeb's

ABOVE: The *Wentworth* at anchor in Newport Harbor on September 17, 1934, with a load of oil drums on deck. *Photo: Roger C. Peterson, collection of the author.* RIGHT: The spectator fleet in Newport Harbor on the 17th, with Fort Adams visible in the far right background. The white arrow indicates the *Alice S. Wentworth*. The Astor yacht *Nourmahal*, on which FDR stayed, is the white vessel second to the left of the *Alice*. *Photo: © Mystic Seaport, Rosenfeld Collection, Mystic, CT.*

fame, as well as his disregard for society, is evident from the invitation that he and Charlie received to go aboard the Vanderbilt yacht for dinner; and which they promptly declined. Many famous yachtsmen did visit the *Alice S. Wentworth*, however, well aware of Zeb's reputation. One of them, who saw him shave the Fort Adams bulkhead, asked why he took such chances with the vessel. "Well, I tell ya. A man born to be hung'll never drown," Zeb replied, certain he'd never die by shipwreck, but might possibly be strung up for other reasons.

The laughter and music from the festivities on board all the yachts echoed merrily through the night. Zeb could party with the best of them, but he had a load of oil drums to move and nothing could stop him—not even a night of revelry in Newport. While most yachtsmen were asleep, or just going to bed, Zeb and the *Alice* left with the tide. He didn't bother to explain that a freighting schooner had to be quick as well as fast and always on the move to make it pay in these changing times.

But even being quick, fast and on the move did not insure against all troubles. On May 12, 1935, Zeb nearly lost a valuable cargo of oysters which he was freighting from New Haven to Chatham. A loosened trunnel which dropped out of the *Wentworth's* planking let in the sea at an alarming rate, and was abetted by a slight leak around the centerboard casing. Zeb's daughter, Rosalie, and his son-in-law, Ed Leonard, pumped feverishly to hold off the on-rushing water, but all in vain. They couldn't keep ahead of it and had to give up. With the assistance of the Coast Guard, Zeb put the *Alice* on the beach near Briton's Cove in Newport. Though Zeb wasn't worried about the safety of his crew, his oysters most certainly couldn't stand the hot sun very long. He fixed the leak himself and hustled into Chatham on time.

The following year brought far greater difficulties. Contracts were to be scarce in 1936, although in January Zeb did agree to move ten ten-thousand-gallon fuel tanks from New Bedford to Nantucket. Two at a time could be carried across the *Wentworth's* deck between the fore and mainmast, leaving just enough room to handle the sails. It was a bitter cold day when they undertook the first load and New Bedford Harbor was completely frozen over. With the yawl boat pushing the vessel to break up the ice and

OPPOSITE: A deck-load of quahaug shells on the *Alice* destined for Nantucket driveways, and cordwood coming out of the hold with the aid of a hoisting engine. RIGHT: Soft coal being unloaded from the deck in Nantucket. BELOW: Zeb, Charlie Sayle and a cargo of oil drums. *All courtesy of Charles F. Sayle.*

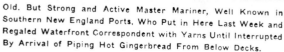

Old. But Strong and Active Master Mariner, Well Known in Southern New England Ports, Who Put in Here Last Week and Regaled Waterfront Correspondent with Yarns Until Interrupted By Arrival of Piping Hot Gingerbread From Below Decks.

LEFT: Zeb as pictured in the July 21, 1935, *Providence Sunday Journal. Courtesy of the Providence Journal Company.* RIGHT: The 1936 New York skyline seen through the rigging of a visiting four-masted schooner. *Photo: Bernice Abbott. Theoline, Pier 11, East River, April 11, 1936. Museum of the City of New York. Federal Art Project—"Changing New York," Abbott file #109.*

the wheel secured, Zeb and Charlie worked from the bow, shoving loose chunks aside by hand. As they passed Palmer's Island in the outer harbor, a man came running out across the ice shouting. It was Mr. Small, the lightkeeper, and he had a fire extinguisher in his hand. Because of their preoccupation with the ice, Zeb and his mate didn't know that the *Wentworth's* cabin was on fire. They both raced aft and Charlie passed buckets of water down to Zeb in the cabin. By the time Mr. Small got aboard, the blaze, which had started in some oily clothes hanging too near the stove, was out. The handsome paneling of which Zeb was so proud had been destroyed and the forward bunks were badly damaged. Zeb continued on to deliver his cargo and when he put back in to Vineyard Haven he could only afford to replace the paneling with plain pine sheathing. Money was scarce.

Zeb's troubles were far from over; his wife had been seriously ill for some time, and in April, 1936, Edith died. As usual, Zeb kept his problems to himself and said little.

Zeb was concerned about his daughter Gertrude, and did express himself on this point. He told the following to a newspaper reporter in Providence. "Two of my daughters are married, but the other one—I don't know—looks like she's due for an old maid, lessen I take some off the stone. When my girls were comin' along of an age to be interested in the boys, I got me a stone, a big one, and set 'er down in the front yard. 'Bout five hundred pounds she weighs. Well, when any of the girls brought a feller to the house asking for her hand, he had to heave up the stone afore I give my permission.

James Cagney. © *Bettman-Corbis Archive.*

"Two of them done it and the girls are married. But the other one, she's still to home. She's had a lot of fellows to the house, but none of them's been able to h'ist the stone. I allus figured a man who couldn't lift five hundred pounds would be no kind of husband for my daughter."

He never got enough off the stone and Gertrude remained unmarried.

By 1936, there were only two vessels in Massachusetts left under commercial sail, and very shortly after that Zeb became the last. There were many who had singled out Zeb as a rare character long before he earned this distinction. Denys Wortman, the famous cartoonist and a Vineyard summer resident, was one. Often he had gone for a sail with Zeb just for the fun of it. In the fall of 1937, Denys, who usually stayed on the Vineyard until late in the year, asked Zeb if he and James Cagney, another regular Vineyard visitor, could sail over to Nantucket with him. The old skipper of course agreed. A load of firewood was already aboard the *Alice* when they arrived at the steamboat wharf in the early morning.

As they climbed aboard, Cagney recalls that Zeb asked him if he knew how to tell the wind direction. Before Cagney could answer, Zeb raised his own right hand, which was black with grime, popped a filthy forefinger in his mouth and held it up, wet and dripping, in the air.

"Well, it ain't like that," said Zeb. "I tell the wind by the way she caresses my cheek—soft and gentle like," and he lightly patted the thorny side of his leathery face.

Although Zeb was nearly seventy-one by then, he still moved about his vessel like a 129

A VIEW OF THE VINEYARD, ALL PHOTOGRAPHED IN 1937 BY ALFRED EISENSTAEDT.

Leo Willoughby (OPPOSITE, TOP LEFT) worked unloading freight from the New Bedford steamer in Edgartown and was a friend of Zeb's, as were Frank Prada and Tony King, the two fishermen in the adjacent picture. A Menemsha fisherman cuts wood (OPPOSITE, BELOW) while another cuts bait (ABOVE). The women (RIGHT) enjoy the morning in their own fashion.

131

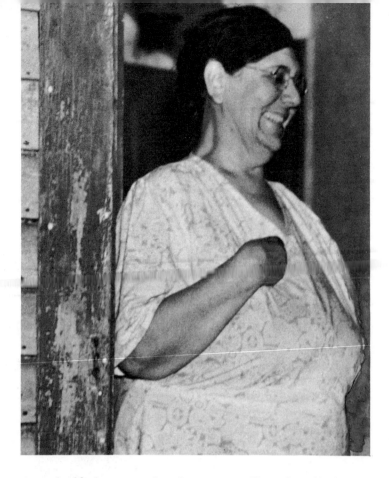

LEFT: Grace McDonald. *The Standard-Times, New Bedford, MA, collection of the author.* OPPOSITE: The *Alice* on a calm sea. *Courtesy of Charles F. Sayle.*

man half the age. As they cast off and sailed out of the harbor, Cagney and Wortman could only be astonished by his handling of the schooner. It was chilly, even for November, and the passengers were bundled in woolen jackets while Zeb stood at the wheel in a thin cotton shirt.

As they rounded East Chop Light, Zeb asked if they'd like some gingerbread and was assured that they did indeed. The mate took the helm and the skipper disappeared below. When he came back on deck, Cagney noticed his hands were unusually white and clean, causing him to wonder if all the dirt was in the cake.

A short time later Zeb went below again and reappeared with the pan of fresh gingerbread as well as some Navy coffee—no percolating—which was consumed without the slightest difficulty while the vessel sailed over the shoals before a cool, brisk wind.

When the firewood was safely delivered, all hands put in to a restaurant for a meal of thick pork chops, corn on the cob and home-fried potatoes. Zeb, by now, had no teeth and when Cagney saw the chops he feared the captain's ability to chew them. As tactfully as possible, he asked Zeb if he could manage the situation. In reply the old man reached over and grabbed the actor's hand and roughly ran it along his upper jaw. It was so sharp it nearly cut Cagney's finger. "Young feller," he snapped, "I can eat anything you can eat," and plunged into the pork.

Zeb began to look increasingly grey and gaunt. Cataracts hindered his vision so that he had to cup his hands around his eyes to focus. But he could still tell his mate that they'd raise a certain buoy in four minutes, and they usually fetched up right on the mark. One knee also bothered him, which he blamed on having been struck by lightning. Though such infirmities would have halted most men his age, Zeb continued to pursue his interests as before.

One day in New Bedford, he decided to look up an old friend, Grace McDonald, now a widow. When the old captain returned to the *Wentworth*, he was all smiles. "She's got all her teeth and not a grey hair in her head, so I asked her to come aboard and cook for us." Zeb liked his women natural—no lipstick, nail polish, rouge or powder. "And she ain't painted like some what look like a chicken that laid an egg too big for its behind." Grace, like every female who knew Zeb, was charmed. A woman in her early sixties, she came from a seafaring family and tipped the scales at nearly two hundred pounds. She was as jolly as she was round.

Grace came along to New Bedford one day in September, 1938, and it was particularly fortunate that Charlie Marthinusen was aboard as well. A hurricane was reported to be zigzagging northeastward at seventeen miles an hour off Florida. What they didn't know was that the storm had been caught in a channel between two high pressure centers and wasn't veering out to sea, but instead was making a straight course towards the North Carolina coast. By the morning of September 21st it was in the vicinity of Cape Hatteras. At 2:30 P.M. Boston radio announced the first warnings and the fringe of the storm hit New York at 2:43. By 3:30, winds of ninety-eight miles per hour had been recorded in New London before the wind cups on the naval anemometer blew away. In a matter of minutes the full fury of the storm hit Rhode Island and Buzzards Bay, pushing seventeen-foot seas before it. By dark, more than three hundred men, women and children in the area were dead. The hurricane was tearing Providence apart and the downtown area was inundated with a ten-foot tide, while out in Narragansett Bay 120-mile-an-hour winds swept the islands clean. A tidal wave rushed in to deal the final blow.

Zeb, Grace and Charlie were in a slip by the Pocahontas coal wharf in New Bed- 133

The aftermath of the 1938 hurricane in New Bedford. *The Standard-Times, New Bedford, MA, collection of the author.*

ford when the storm hit. The dock lines were tied to spiles, but with the rapidly rising water, Zeb and Charlie knew they wouldn't hold. Charlie got into the dory, in the teeth of the storm, and while he put a smaller line on a spile to hold it temporarily, he took the larger line and tied it on some iron bits near the coal cars. The vessel then had bow and stern, port and starboard lines holding her. The water continued to rise until it was six feet above the wharf. The *Wentworth* had a few scratches from debris but she was one of only a handful of vessels in New Bedford to survive the storm. News of ships, missing along the coast with all hands, was reported for weeks afterward.

At the same time, Zeb's debts were mounting and it was getting increasingly difficult to make his schooner pay. The oyster business went to power boats in 1938. The *Wentworth's* menus were reduced to the barest essentials. If a lobster pot was fouled, the contents were "borrowed" and all had a good feed. On one trip out of Vineyard Haven when they had only a few staples aboard, Zeb decided he had to have a really tasty meal. He dropped anchor off Naushon and told Charlie he'd row ashore and dig a few clams for chowder.

Zeb pulled the dory up on the beach and then, instead of clams, he picked up a big rock, and started walking cautiously across a field toward a large flock of sheep. Roast lamb was surely on his mind. As Charlie watched, Zeb knocked one of the unsuspecting animals on the head, threw it over his shoulder and brought it back on board. "I don't think they'll miss one, do you Charlie?" he asked. They feasted on roast lamb, lamb chops, lamb stew and cold lamb. It lasted for two weeks. As Zeb put it, "We ate everything but the bleat."

But hard times had come to stay. Finally Zeb's debts reached the point where the *Alice S. Wentworth* had to be attached by his creditors. The man who had managed, all through the Depression, to keep himself and many others provided with life's necessities, who had lent money widely which was never returned, and who was considered indomitable in every way, seemed to be washed up on the shore at last. Zeb was proud, but perplexed. "Is it such a terrible thing a man should be broke? Hasn't anyone ever gotten himself into this kind of a hole before?" he asked defensively.

The starboard side of the *Wentworth*, loaded with cordwood and tacking out of Fairhaven. *Photo: C.B. Mitchell, courtesy of South Street Seaport Museum.*

VII
WEDDING SAILS

On January 15, 1939, the U.S. Marshal came down from Boston to post the notice on her mainmast, and after fifty-nine years at sea, Zeb went on the beach. He was, perhaps, a man who truly loves only once in a lifetime, and the *Alice S. Wentworth* had held his affection since the first time he set eyes on her. For eighteen years she had been his whole life. To many besides Zeb, she had become a symbol, a lonely reminder of those glorious days of working sail. Now the schooner lay idle alongside the steamboat wharf, her hatches and companionway inhospitably closed, her old canvas neatly furled.

Zeb was quiet, but without any trace of bitterness. He realized the vessel's fate lay on the auction block, and for a month he lived with his daughter Ruth, awaiting that awful event in mid-February.

The day loomed up cloudy and cold, bleak enough to match the old skipper's mood. Word had spread on the island that Zeb and his vessel were to be separated, and about fifty people gathered around. Dan Chapman, the Deputy Marshal who acted as auctioneer, came off the noon boat and stood on the back of a truck alongside where the *Wentworth* lay. Her scarred and blistered decks and rotting rigging made her look nearly as forlorn as her captain.

A Greenport skipper who had lost his own vessel in the 1938 hurricane opened the bidding at four hundred dollars. The second bid was $425, and the third $500. Then S.C. Luce of Vineyard Haven raised it to $501 and the dollar ante for a seventy-three-foot schooner began.

"I doubt if the judge will like this," the auctioneer grumbled at such a highly irregular procedure. "I'll get fired when I get back to Boston." Several men then went into a huddle.

"Now it looks like a conspiracy," he complained.

"That's just what it is," someone called. "The *Wentworth* ain't goin' to the mainland."

After a few more bids the schooner was knocked down to Captain Ralph Packer for $701, who then announced to Zeb that he was to remain as captain. Zeb mumbled a quiet thanks and stepped back aboard. The auctioneer seemed glad to get back on the ferry.

Captain Packer had conceived the idea of selling shares at ten dollars each in order to keep the *Wentworth* freighting. Subscription letters were sent out and brought an immediate response. James Cagney; Denys Wortman; Katherine Cornell; Dr. Stanley 137

The *Alice S. Wentworth* being overhauled.
BELOW: The bowsprit gets a new coat of paint
while Charlie Marthinusen (OPPOSITE)
restores her name on the trailboards.
OVERLEAF: Zeb supervises the painting of the
deck by two of his grandsons. *Photos: A.B.
Merry.*

King, the president of Amherst; Mr. Calvin Child, a director of RCA and Victor; Dr. Frank Jewett of AT&T; Griswold Lorillard, tobacco heir of Tuxedo Park; Charles Sayle of Nantucket; Vineyard merchants and Zeb's friends all bought shares in the schooner. Judge Arthur Davis of Edgartown was appointed president, Ralph Packer, treasurer and Stephen C. Luce, clerk.

The claims against the schooner were quickly settled and Zeb was put on a monthly salary. Charlie Marthinusen went as mate, and Grace McDonald found her way back to the galley. They made a few trips at once, but as soon as the weather eased, the shareholders' money was used to restore the pride and joy of the Alice S. Wentworth Associates.

Older men who remembered the art of overhauling a fore-and-after were sought for the work. Frank Canha was selected to hew the new topmasts; Elmer Chadwick, the village blacksmith, forged new chain plates and repaired the dead-eyes. Charlie Marthinusen climbed aloft to rig a new foretopmast and the finest of steam-tarred hemp was used for the lanyards in her standing rigging. A bright gold ball graced the main truck and new hoops and halyards were rigged and rove off for the new gaff topsail. She was painted as smooth as the sides of a fish.

Zeb was his old self again. Though a bit stooped and using his knees more to lift huge weights, his spirits were higher than ever. At seventy-two, he was bursting with energy and enthusiasm.

"I figger I'm in such good shape," he told reporters who pursued him in every port, "'cause I never smoked or drank. But I worked hard. Lord knows there ain't a man on the Vineyard worked any harder. But I took care of myself, and look at me now. 'Course I ain't lived on butterfly wings and wind puddin'; I've always had plenty of good grub."

And on the subject of the *Wentworth* he reported, "I've got half the yachtsmen on the coast looking at me with envy right now. And I wa'n't say I blame them. I've got 'em licked for looks and speed," and he patted the wheel. "In fact, this here is my car, too. She'll support twenty persons, whereas a car will keep twenty broke. I did have a car once't but a boy of mine run wild in it and capsized the rig. I ain't had one since."

Daylight Savings Time seemed to be his main source of irritation these days. The issue had been hotly contested in the Massachusetts legislature and some years earlier petitions were circulated on the island that had soundly defeated the idea of tampering 139

with the clock. "The tide was here before Daylight Savings was, and if it be good enough for the tide, it be good enough for me. Keep on changing the clock around and a man'll be back from Delaware with a load of oysters 'fore he's gotten under way to go after 'em. What good be this new time anyway? You hire a gang to work for you and all they do with that extra hour in the morning is spend it picking their teeth and putting their overalls on. And then, before the sun is up over the foreyard, it be time to quit!"

The tale of the auction, Zeb's reputation and the fact that the *Alice* was the last commercial cargo carrier under sail in southern New England, found Zeb the center of attention wherever he went. The thorny veteran accepted it all with nonchalance and good humor, although he would have preferred to have been left alone. Zeb was entirely content to simply keep moving freight, see his friends, and stand at the wheel for hours on end talking to himself and to *Alice*. They hauled cordwood, lumber, coal, scrap iron, an occasional load of furniture, road oil, even automobiles (when there was a ferry strike), if fact, anything that could fit on the *Wentworth's* deck.

On August 15th of the following year, the Alice S. Wentworth Associates had their first stockholders' meeting aboard the schooner. Many people were invited, including the editor of the Nantucket paper, who refused. When an effort was made to change his mind, for the sake of local color, he replied curtly, "Perhaps the Vineyard needs local color. Nantucket does not." Zeb was dressed in a stovepipe hat and frock coat for the event. It was just a bit theatrical; akin to the placing of whale oil casks on the schooner's deck for her ill-fated movie debut years before. Zeb went along with the fun good-naturedly, content that he could sail her the way he wanted all the rest of the year. Officers reported the financial success of their venture and declared a one-dollar dividend. Thirteen hundred dollars had put the schooner in fine shape and she was actually showing a profit. With her new ensign flying from the main truck, tables for lunch and plenty of deck chairs were set along the rails on both sides of the waist. Everyone chatted gaily as they ate and then went for a sail over towards Falmouth and back.

There was a larger price Zeb had to pay for his fame. Romantic gossip was in the air at each port he touched. Reporters pursued him night and day, though Zeb could fend them off as easily as he used to handle a keg of nails. Grace, like every woman who was ever close to Zeb, hoped the rumors were true. She smiled, cooked and scrubbed.

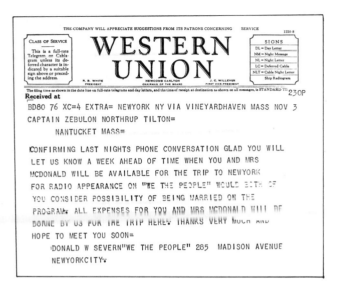

LEFT: Lowell Thomas broadcasting his nightly newscast. *Courtesy of NBC.* ABOVE and OPPOSITE: The correspondence relating to Zeb's appearance on "We the People," in 1939. *Courtesy of Rosalie Tilton Spence.*

Whenever the old vessel came up through Hell Gate and slid down the East River, rounded Brandt Point off Nantucket, or sailed into New Bedford, reporters were on hand to query him about his future plans.

"They asked me in Nantucket 'tother day when I was gettin' married. Well, the fact is, I ain't." But the press wouldn't settle for that. In September, Zeb finally relented enough to say that maybe sometime he and Grace would tend to the matter, though he wasn't in any rush himself. "She'll just have to wait a bit. I got a lot of work to do yet and if she won't wait, well, women are like trolleys, two or three more'll be around in no time. After all, you're tying a knot with your tongue which you can't untie with your teeth."

By the end of October he couldn't suppress the news any longer. Reporters discovered that a new mainsail was being cut and sewn for the *Wentworth* at a loft in Fairhaven to celebrate a wedding. Zeb had also asked several friends to sign affidavits to prove he'd been legally divorced from his first wife forty years earlier, since he had been refused a marriage license until this point was cleared up. Several friends signed papers drawing attention to Edith Mayhew and their seven children as proof of his second marriage in Oak Bluffs. Though he tried to brush all questions aside, on October 10th, the whole world knew. On his nightly coast-to-coast newscast, Lowell Thomas gave the formal announcement of Zeb's engagement to Grace McDonald.

When the bridegroom-to-be sailed over to New Bedford one day at the end of October, the event appeared imminent. It surely seemed so to the bride. But Zeb put her off, too. "Zebulon, you said we'd be married by Christmas," she reminded him.

"Yus," he replied, "but I ain't said which Christmas."

Nevertheless Grace was an optimistic soul. "My furniture and other belongings are all packed in burlap bags ready to go aboard the schooner," she reminded reporters. Her

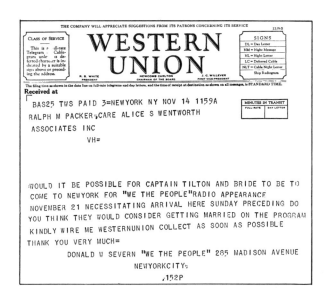

Received at

BAS25 TWS PAID 3=NEWYORK NY NOV 14 1159A

RALPH M PACKER,CARE ALICE S WENTWORTH

ASSOCIATES INC

VH=

MINUTES IN TRANSIT
FULL-RATE   DAY LETTER

WOULD IT BE POSSIBLE FOR CAPTAIN TILTON AND BRIDE TO BE TO
COME TO NEWYORK FOR "WE THE PEOPLE"RADIO APPEARANCE
NOVEMBER 21 NECESSITATING ARRIVAL HERE SUNDAY PRECEDING DO
YOU THINK THEY WOULD CONSIDER GETTING MARRIED ON THE PROGRAM
KINDLY WIRE ME WESTERNUNION COLLECT AS SOON AS POSSIBLE
THANK YOU VERY MUCH=

DONALD W SEVERN "WE THE PEOPLE" 285 MADISON AVENUE

NEWYORKCITY,

.152P

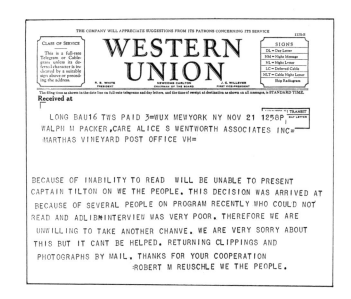

Received at

LONG BAU16 TWS PAID 3=WUX MEWYORK NY NOV 21 1258P

WALPH M PACKER,CARE ALICE S WENTWORTH ASSOCIATES INC=
MARTHAS VINEYARD POST OFFICE VH=

BECAUSE OF INABILITY TO READ WILL BE UNABLE TO PRESENT
CAPTAIN TILTON ON WE THE PEOPLE. THIS DECISION WAS ARRIVED AT
BECAUSE OF SEVERAL PEOPLE ON PROGRAM RECENTLY WHO COULD NOT
READ AND ADLIBN INTERVIEW WAS VERY POOR. THEREFORE WE ARE
UNWILLING TO TAKE ANOTHER CHANVE. WE ARE VERY SORRY ABOUT
THIS BUT IT CANT BE HELPED. RETURNING CLIPPINGS AND
PHOTOGRAPHS BY MAIL. THANKS FOR YOUR COOPERATION
ROBERT M REUSCHLE WE THE PEOPLE.

raisin-colored wedding dress was in readiness on a hanger at the far side of her room, close by the west window which faced out on the harbor.

A few days later when he was loading his vessel in New Bedford, Zeb allowed as how they would be married in the Seamen's Bethel in Vineyard Haven. "It'll be a free-for-all; there won't be no secrets about any of it and anybody can come what wants to. There'll be plenty of coffee and cake, entertainment and music, so's everybody will have a good time. One man wanted us to be married at 2 P.M., but I said Lord, no! That's a funeral hour and neither of us is dead yet. I think it's more 'n likely we'll be married around 3 P.M., 'cause that's when the Nantucket steamer pulls in and all the crew want to attend. And I'm goin' to ask Mr. Thurber (Reverend Charles Thurber) to see if he can come down here to marry us. He always does a good job of it. We'll stand at the wheel—her holding one spike and me the other." Again reporters pressed him for an exact date and again he avoided answering.

"I've got to take a load of coal and wood to Nantucket first, then the vessel needs her new dress for the wedding and a little fixing up. And I'm gonna get me a new blue serge suit. Then I got to get spruced up a little. I'm a homely lookin' cuss and it'll take a little something. No, we ain't gettin' married this Saturday."

On November 14, Donald Severn of "We the People" radio program, one of the first national personal interview programs, wired Zeb. He was invited to come to New York and appear on the program. Captain Ralph Packer and his wife helped to make the necessary arrangements, which were momentarily cancelled when the program director discovered that Zeb couldn't read very well, especially since his cataracts had become worse. Mrs. Packer hastily assured them Zeb's personality would come through under any conditions and he was re-invited.

His new suit would do fine for both the trip and for the wedding. When he strode

Burgess Meredith, who interviewed Zeb on "We the People." *Burgess Meredith ©Bettman–Corbis Archive.* OPPOSITE: Various newspaper accounts of the romance.

down to the Vineyard Haven wharf to take the ferry, friends who had come to see him off hardly recognized the old man. It wasn't the haircut, the suit or the newly shined high black shoes, but the overcoat—the first one he'd ever owned. For those who had only seen him in his usual boots-and-suspenders rig, it was quite a shock. Zeb also carried a small black bag which Mrs. Packer had loaned him for the event. Just before he stepped on the ferry, Captain Packer asked him what was in the bag. Zeb snapped it open. Crumpled in the corner lay one red necktie.

They drove to Boston and then took the train to New York. The city was quite a novelty to Zeb, who wasn't familiar with any part of it except the waterfront. He stayed at the Commodore Hotel and was guest of honor at a small dinner. Zeb really didn't much like the radio interview, which was conducted by Burgess Meredith. From the questions asked, it was apparent that Meredith did not realize the *Alice* was a subject far more fascinating to the old man than his much publicized romance with Grace, about which he was repeatedly questioned. As usual, he took it all good-naturedly, but was clearly glad to get back to the Vineyard.

"They cook meat down there so's a man can't eat it," he explained to his daughter, "and they put it on a plate with bulkheads. I like mine crisped up, so when the waiter brung it to me I asked him about his stove. He said 'twas cooked on electricity, so I told him to take it back and give it another shock. But 'twas no good anyway. And the bed was so soft I had to get up and walk 'round 'tother side when I wanted to turn over."

The radio interview brought fan letters from all over. The *Vineyard Gazette* reported Zeb's voice had come over loud and clear and sounded very natural. Reporters still followed him, but Zeb stalled them again about the wedding.

"Guess I'll just have to wait 'til the harbor freezes over. I've got plenty of work now. Too busy loading at the moment. Won't be out of here until Monday on the turn of the tide."

On through December he continued freighting. Grace didn't go with him in winter, but waited patiently in her house. Finally, in the first week of January, the wedding day was announced. When Zeb made up his mind, he took quick action. They'd be married almost immediately, on Saturday, January 13, at 3 P.M. in the Seamen's Bethel, just after the Nantucket boat pulled in. The first wedding present—ten pounds of coffee—arrived right after the announcement.

146

Sailmakers Prepare New 'Dress' for Wentworth

BLACK LISTED

Flt # 719

Bos - Sfo

6:16 - 12:15

'Zeb' Tilton Will Be Married At Wheel of His Vessel Here

Some one of these days a rugged green schooner with a touch of aristocracy will come beating up the Bay. Off Butler's Flat, or thereabouts, she'll douse most of her canvas and a snub-nosed yawl-boat with an over-sized kicker will shove the vessel into Union Wharf, Fairhaven. And when that happens, the bridegroom will have arrived.

Because that's the way Captain Zebulon "Zeb" Northrop Tilton, 72, is coming when he arrives to claim his bride, Mrs. Grace McDonald, 62, of 25 Water Street, Fairhaven.

The marriage, formerly set for Friday, was unable to take place because bad weather kept Zeb and the schooner Alice S. Wentworth in Vineyard Haven. But the bride was undaunted by that and quoted the old saying about mice and men.

To Come From Vineyard

"The ___ ___ come from Vine-
the s___ as he can," she

an edge of a newly completed sail is Ralph W. Silsby. Seated (center) is Miss Jennie Palmer and Raymond F. Brunettte is shown at right.

killed seamstresses to ___ to-be. Women skilled ___ been selected to make ___ the wedding of Cap-___ and Mrs. Grace Mac-exception to the rule. (When,

new ___ tain Zeb Tilton ___ Donald is not going to be an as and if.)

You've heard often of the bridal veil, but in this case, it's the bridal sail that's attracting most attention of all the "garments" in the trousseau, because the schooner Alice S. Wentworth is going to have a new mainsail for the nuptials.

"We're going to be married der the schooner's 'new dress' Zeb confided, "and the Wentworth new dress is considerably more expensive than the bride's new dress will be."

The mainsail, all roped and ready to be bent on, is lying in Ralph W. Silsby's sail loft in Fairhaven now, waiting for Zeb and the vessel to arrive next week. Forty-five feet on the foot, 55 on the leach and 38 on the luff, Mr. Silsby says, "It's the biggest sail I've made since I went into business here in 1932." Four hundred yards of No. 3 duck

went into the sail, which was finished Thursday.

But don't forget the feminine touch so necessary to the preparation of all parts of the tr___ even the bridal sai___ Palmer, sail___ choice ___

Captain Zeb Tilton on Way To Meet Bride in Fairhaven

Special to Standard-Times

VINEYARD HAVEN, Oct. 10—Spring and romance filled the air, despite the date on the calendar, as Captain 'Zeb' Tilton, 72, stood at the wheel of his schooner the Alice S. Wentworth and sailed out of this harbor at 7 this morning before a light south easterly breeze.

Bound for Fairhaven, in the third attempt to see his sweetheart, Mrs. Grace McDonald, weather conditions appeared more favorable today than those which canceled ___ poiseti ___ with ___

it plain that her answer will be "yes" and Zeb figures that maybe they'll be married Saturday aboard the vessel. Some rumors ___ that the couple ___

Sils' ___ ointed to a youth at the ___ busy over a piece bac___ of

'Maybe in 2 Saturdays,' Skipper Zeb Declares Of His Marriage Plans

NANTUCKET, Oct. 19 — The wedding of Captain Zeb Tilton and his bride-to-be, Mrs. Grace McDonald, formerly of Fairhaven, won't be this Saturday, "but maybe in two Saturdays," Zeb said today.

The best man will be Charles Sayle of Nantucket, model boat builder, Tilton said. Mr. Sayle raises a beard each Winter, regardless of weddings.

It will be a single ring ceremony. "Only women wear jewelry," Zeb said scornfully today. "Men don't wear the stuff."

Mrs. McDonald's furniture still ___ oard the schooner Alice S. ___ orth; the couple are sailing ___ ck to New Bedford soon ___ nother load of coal and fig- ___ on unloading it at Nantuck- ___ and then going to Vineyard ___ aven where the wedding is to ___ place ___

ure is packe ___ bags and p ___ ___ ment- ___ ___ rking of ___ ___ ker sai ___ witho ___

Amusements

Ends Today: STANLEY & ___
STONE & ___

are Today ___

OPPOSITE: Zeb and Grace in October of 1939 and (RIGHT) before the wheel of the *Alice* in the Seamen's Bethel on January 13, 1940. *The Standard-Times, New Bedford, MA.*

The event attracted more attention than anything that had taken place in the town for years. The press, Zeb's friends and the curious gathered long before the appointed hour. The small Seamen's Bethel was packed to overflowing, while more crowds clustered around outside the windows to watch. Among the well-wishers were three generations of nautical veterans of both sail and steam. The Bethel was decorated with greenery; ship paintings lined the walls, and ship models decorated the mantle and piano. The *Wentworth's* wheel was taken off the vessel and placed upright by the altar, flanked on either side by potted plants. White streamers and bells were suspended above the head of the nuptial pair.

Just ten minutes before the ceremony commenced, the island steamer *Nantucket* rounded the Vineyard Haven breakwater. Captain James C. Sandsbury and his crew raced ashore just in time for the service, which, in the end, delayed the ferry's scheduled departure.

As Zeb and Charlie were standing in the waiting room to the left of the altar, Zeb drew the minister aside for a word of caution. "Don't ask me to promise too much," he warned him.

Moments later, at the stroke of three, the chaplain struck six bells on a ship's gong, signifying the time and change of watch. Zeb and Charlie stepped forward from the right to face the minister. Grace, in her raisin-colored dress, attended by Zeb's daughter Rosalie wearing black with red trim, stepped forward from the left. At the appropriate moment, Rosalie's little blond daughter came forward with the ring.

There were refreshments and two wedding cakes, one of which Zeb's old friend Charlie Sayle had brought along from Nantucket. Asked where they'd go on their honeymoon, Zeb said they'd take a little trip over to New Bedford and pick up a load of coal for Nantucket.

When the festivities were over, the ferry crew hurried back to the pier. On its way out of the harbor, the *Nantucket* sounded three blasts in salute to the happy couple. The *Wentworth's* wheel was put back on the schooner, and as the wind came up Zeb and Grace put to sea amid cheers from the onlookers.

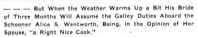
— — — But When the Weather Warms Up a Bit His Bride of Three Months Will Assume the Galley Duties Aboard the Schooner Alice S. Wentworth, Being, in the Opinion of Her Spouse, "a Right Nice Cook."

OPPOSITE: The *Alice* and her captain, with ever-present coffee mugs by the wheel, and the yawl boat up on davits, photographed in 1939 by Samuel Chamberlain. *Courtesy Peabody Essex Museum.* ABOVE: A newspaper clipping from the *Providence Journal. Courtesy of the Providence Sunday Journal Company.* Two snapshots of Zeb's guests (mostly female, as usual) during a sailing party. *Photos: Charles F. Sayle.* RIGHT: Zeb and his youngest son Harold pulling the *Alice* alongside the pier. *The Standard-Times, New Bedford, MA, collection of the author.*

Interest in Zeb and in his celebrated wedding, plus the fact that his first appearance had been such a success, generated another invitation for he and Grace to broadcast again. They went to New York at the end of January and were interviewed a second time on "We the People."

Despite such notoriety, Zeb continued to crisscross southern New England carrying his freights, with Grace going along in all but the coldest weather. By now, ominous grey warships filled the coastal waterways. The sight of the elderly schooner sailing along with her old captain at the helm must have made many a young Navy man long for the simpler era which Zeb and *Alice* seemed to represent.

The war didn't seem to effect Zeb at all, except for the strict clearance rules now being enforced at each port. According to him, he'd been through six of them anyway: "I sailed a vessel in the Spanish-American War, World War 1 and I'm sailing in this one. Added to that I've been married three times—that makes six wars, don't it?"

The war did cause some change in his cargoes, though not in the way they were moved. The old man still believed in the wind. "It's the one thing that don't go up in price, and besides, it ain't rationed. A man should use these things." 151

"I was just thinking, Clem, there ain't any old timers anymore. We're them now."

In August, 1941, there was the All-Island Cavalcade for the benefit of the Martha's Vineyard Hospital; part circus, agricultural fair, horse and art show. Zeb had freighted in the brick for the hospital and was on hand to have his portrait painted. Hundreds were able to watch none other than Thomas Hart Benton at work, for whom Zeb posed stiffly, and for once, according to Benton, wordlessly. Zeb was not a man well suited to sitting still. The cavalcade produced a veritable pantheon of artistic celebrities. Denys Wortman was there and produced cartoons for a dollar apiece, and George Brehm sold quick oil portraits for five dollars each. Sanford Low and Harwood Steiger also worked in oils. Gilbert Bundy, the widely published cartoonist, generously contributed some of his work as well.

Several famous Vineyarders besides Zeb also appeared, including Captain Hartson Bodfish, the famous whaler; Amos Smalley, a Gay Head Indian, the only Vineyarder to harpoon a white whale; Chief Black Hawk; and Mr. and Mrs. Napolean Bonaparte Madison. At the softball game Katherine Cornell pitched, ably assisted by Mr. Wortman and Mr. Benton, among others. Thus the summer ended on a gay and colorful note. Zeb

OPPOSITE: A coasting schooner at sunset. *Photo: Joseph B. Hale, courtesy of the Vineyard Gazette.* ABOVE: The transom of the *Alice S. Wentworth. Courtesy of Charles F. Sayle.*

was firmly established in his own way among the most celebrated individuals of the day. Yet it was ironic that such a conclusion to the season served also as a prelude to the end of the very part of his life from which his fame had sprung.

In 1942, after sixty years in the coastwise schooner trade, Zeb finally went ashore for an operation on his eyes. Although he didn't realize it at the time, he would never sail the *Alice* again. For so many years she had been his whole life, his only true mistress. Whatever premonitions he may have felt he kept to himself. Without a word, he packed his bag and walked off the wharf, his familiar port-and-starboard rolling gait carrying him on up Main Street.

EPILOGUE

The Alice S. Wentworth Associates continued operating the schooner for another two years. Without Zeb, however, it could never be the same, and the members voted reluctantly to sell her down east. The *Alice* sailed away from the Vineyard as a cargo vessel for the last time in July 1943, and Zeb was there to see her off. The new skipper, Capt. Parker Hall, had some difficulty getting her under way, and at one point nearly went up on the beach. "See? She don't want to leave without me," Zeb explained.

Zeb's wife Grace had been hospitalized on the Vineyard in 1941, so he went to stay with Rosalie, who lived in Middleboro. Zeb's eye operation had been a success, though the period of recuperation was considerably longer than Zeb would have liked. The improvement of his vision, however, seemed to restore much of the old man's wit, energy and restless need to get moving. Zeb decided, at the age of seventy-seven, to go coasting again.

In 1944 he bought himself a small, old two-master that lay rotting on the New Bedford waterfront. The *Coral* had been damaged in the 1936 hurricane, but with wartime rationing, travel restrictions and military priorities, Zeb felt sure there would still be plenty of calls to move things his way. The prospects were promising.

"The wind still ain't rationed," was Zeb's comment, as he set to work overhauling the little vessel.

But with Grace's continued illness and his own medical bills, money was scarce and work on the schooner was slow. When she was hauled out of the water in Fairhaven, her condition was found to be much worse than Zeb had realized. Still, his time was his own and he continued to travel between Fairhaven and the island, where he now stayed with various members of his family—George Fred, Ruth or Gertrude. For Zeb, these were happy, casual days, unhurried and filled with plans for the future.

After spending seven years in the hospital, Grace died in 1948. Zeb continued to be active. In 1950, however, he fell and broke his hip. Once again he went to live with Rosalie in Middleboro. People still dropped in to sit by the fire and chat about his years at sea, for even in such condition, he was as full of wit and wisdom as ever. It was inevitable, of course, that his health would eventually begin to fail. Although it wasn't detected immediately, the old skipper, it turned out, had cancer, and on February 28, 1952, at the age of eighty-five, he died, bringing an end to a legendary life and to an era as well.

The ending of the voyage. ABOVE, LEFT: Zeb recuperating at Rosalie's home in Middleboro, Massachusetts, in 1941. ABOVE: Zeb in 1944 at the wheel of his new vessel, the *Coral. Both, The Standard—Times, New Bedford, MA.* LEFT: The 1961 brochure offering vacation cruises on the *Alice. Collection of the author.* BELOW: The *Alice* going to Boston to be berthed beside Pier 4. *Courtesy of Anthony Athanas, collection of the author.*

Sail The
Alice
Wentworth

Zeb and a lady friend sailing off Nantucket. *Photo: Charles F. Sayle.*

Perhaps Zeb was too plain a figure for the fancy words said about him after his death, though he most surely was indeed "a stronger and braver Cyrano, a wittier and leaner Falstaff." Still, a remark he made to Jack Jenkinson, shortly before he died, was perhaps more his style. "I don't regret nothin'," said Zeb, "and the girls still love me."

As for the *Alice,* with Capt. Parker Hall at the helm, she sailed on in Maine waters, moving brick, coal, lumber and other cargoes. After ten years the schooner was sold at auction. The *Alice* changed owners several more times and sailed as a windjammer cruise ship. She was based in Woods Hole when once again she went on the auction block. Anthony Athanas, owner of Anthony's Pier 4 Restaurant in Boston, bought her for $13,500 in 1965. She lay alongside his restaurant as an attraction and reminder of Boston's history of oar and sail.

A few years after, she began to deteriorate badly and Athanas offered to give the vessel to an organization that planned to have her hauled and restored. Plans were pretty well along when, in 1974, an April gale struck the Boston area and Zeb's beloved *Alice* was wrecked beyond repair. She was 111 years old.

Old Zeb

I'm not tired of the wind;
I'm not weary of the sea.
But she's prob'ly had her belly full
Of a damned old coot like me.
I'm goin' ashore;
She's gone for better days.
But I'll see her topsail flyin'
When I come down off the ways.

 Rosie, get my Sunday shoes;
 Gertie, get my walking cane,
 We'll take another walk to see
 Old Alice sail again.

I'd like to have a nickel
For the men I used to know
Who could load three cord of lumber
In half an hour or so
Who could put on sail by haulin',
'Stead of donkeying around.
Then I'd be the poorest coasterman
This side of Edgartown.

 Rosie, get my Sunday shoes . . .

Any fool can work an engine!
Takes brains to work a sail,
And I never seen no steamer
Make much good out of a gale.
You can go and pay your taxes
For the rationed gas you get,
But at least to me, the wind is free
And they haven't run out yet.

 Rosie, get my Sunday shoes . . .

If I ever get back to her,
You know I'll treat her just the same,
I'll jibe her when I want to, boys,
And I'll sail in freezing rain,
I'll park old Alice on the beach
And go dancin' in the town,
'Cause a man who's fit for hanging
Prob'ly never will get drowned.

 Rosie, get my Sunday shoes . . .

Words and music by Larry Kaplan
Copyright 1977
Hannah Lane Music, BMI